Celebrate

How to cre
personali:

Jane Patmore
Foreword by Angie Alexandra

Ceremony
Books

Published in 2016 by Ceremony Books

ISBN Paperback: 978-0-9956334-0-7
Ebook: 978-0-9956334-1-4

A CIP catalogue copy of this book can be found in the British Library.

Published with the help of Indie Authors World

IndieAuthors
World

*'Hi Jane, Our ceremony was beautiful! Thank you so,
so much for your lovely words, it's made the wedding so personal.
Everybody commented, saying how lovely it was.
We had such an amazing day.'*

Laura and Denholm

*'Hi Jane, That is a lovely, lovely service, and we are extremely happy
with it. It felt like a close friend was writing it!'*

Georgina and Dave

*'Hi Jane, The ceremony is so lovely, thank you! We really
love the way that you have captured our desire to include reference to
both our past and our future, as well as all of the little bits and pieces
that we had picked out.'*

Janette and Stuart

*'Dear Jane, just a note to say thank you so very much for all your help,
hard work, and for marrying us. You delivered the most beautiful and
personal service and we will be forever grateful for this.'*

Shelley and Gordon

*'Our warmest thanks for providing us with such a
beautiful ceremony – it was so very personal, and evoked much
happiness. We have a superb photo of us drinking out of the quaich,
every time we look at it, it makes us laugh and fills us with
warm happy memories. Thank you so very much.'*

Ian and Claire

*'What an amazing day! Fabulous wedding ceremony,
acknowledging all the elements we had suggested, but then
built into a fabulous ceremony which was everything that we had
dreamed of and more. So grateful for all the hard work, and the ease
with which you ensured everything went without a hitch. It was so
moving, there was hardly a dry eye in the house. Xxx'*

Al & Ali

Contents

Acknowledgements

I appreciate the support and help of everyone who has encouraged me to write this book, my friends, my colleagues, and my family, and I am grateful for all the examples which have been offered to me by other celebrants who are also involved in such wonderful work. However, most of all I want to express my heartfelt thanks to the many couples who have shared their stories and their words. Without their love for each other and their desire to express their feelings in a personal way, none of this would have been possible. Thank you. I feel honoured to have been a part of your lives.

I have put this book together trusting that I am helping and supporting couples and also their celebrants. However, I am aware of the finite lexicon when we try to write about love and marriage. The words used and the examples given have all come from marriage ceremonies that I have held. Sometimes they are words which I have put together, and sometimes I have included phrases which couples have offered to me. On the latter, I cannot know the source. It is never my intention to claim someone else's work as my own, and if you feel this has happened inadvertently, then please let me know so I can make amendments.

There's always a question that people like to ask a celebrant – who would you choose and trust to hold your own wedding? Well, when I was married, I chose Angie Alexandra to be my celebrant. She is a trusted mentor, an inspiration, a source of knowledge, and a good friend. So I was thrilled and a little awestruck when she offered to contribute the Foreword to this book, and to add some case studies and final thoughts, giving her own perspective. Thank you, Angie, for this work.

About the Author

Jane Patmore is an Interfaith Celebrant, and has held hundreds of wedding ceremonies for couples who want to make sure that their wedding ceremony is personal, unique, and reflects what is important to them. Jane believes that every wedding is special, no matter how large or small, elaborate or simple.

Any couple planning to get married can find lots of advice on the internet, but there is nowhere that pulls all the information together as comprehensively as this book. Jane has used her years of experience to provide a step-by-step guide to help to make your wedding personal and unique.

Jane, who lives near Edinburgh, has enjoyed a varied career in research, management, training, coaching, and personal development. She loves working with people and has a talent for being able to listen to what people really want to say, then recreating that in the form of a ceremony which is both personal and meaningful.

Jane trained with the Interfaith Foundation and, through her association with them, is authorised to perform the legal aspects of a wedding ceremony in Scotland. She offers a full range of services, from helping couples to plan and write their ceremony to conducting the event for them. Jane is happy to travel across Scotland, the UK, or the world, to help people create amazing ceremonies.

If you would like Jane to help you create your wedding ceremony, or if you would like her to conduct your wedding (including the legal ceremony in Scotland), you can contact her on jane@yourserviceinscotland.co.uk

Foreword by Angie Alexandra

I'm delighted to support and commend this book. My path first crossed with Jane's when she telephoned to enquire about the possibility of me holding her forthcoming marriage ceremony, and at that point, neither of us had any idea how our chance meeting would impact both our lives. Not only did I have the honour of marrying Jane and her husband Derek, but Jane was so inspired by what she could enjoy for her wedding ceremony that she embarked upon the training to become a celebrant herself.

As a result of Jane's hard work in making interfaith ceremonies more visible out in the world, more and more couples have heard about and discovered how flexible and personal they can be, and have realised that an interfaith wedding ceremony might be a good fit for them.

There are lots of books on the market about weddings, but none quite like this one. It's a great pleasure for me to commend this book, not only because of my friendship and working relationship with Jane, but because this book is so thoughtful and thorough. This book is all about the options and choices you have, so you can make informed decisions about what your ceremony will include on possibly the most memorable day of your life. Maybe the date is decided and the venue booked, the photographer chosen, and the dress ordered. Many of the key aspects of your day are in place already, giving you a window to think about who is going to guide you through the process, create your ceremony with you, hold your ceremony on the day and officiate during the legal aspects of marriage. This book offers practical advice and will inspire and help you, and your chosen celebrant, to consider all the different elements for your ceremony and work through the possibilities to help create your perfect day.

Based on a tried and tested format of information and questions that Jane sends to couples when she is working with them, this book takes you on a journey through planning your ceremony. It starts with an overview detailing everything you might want to think about before your ceremony actually begins; it shows how to create a personal ceremony right from the start, setting the right atmosphere and gaining clarity on the purpose; it guides you through the process of recounting your own story, the journey from meeting to the point of marriage, your hopes and dreams for the future, and the shared values on which you'll base your relationship; and it offers advice on how to structure your vows and find the perfect combination of words and phrases to create meaningful and personal vows and promises.

The internet gives us access to many examples of ritual and symbolic gesture, but in this book Jane helps you to better understand some of the meaning, and why you might choose a particular ritual or gesture, and she also offers ideas for creating something more unusual and unique to you. There is a wealth of practical advice on other content such as music, readings, and ways in which to involve your family and friends in the ceremony.

So wherever your ceremony will be held, and whether your wedding will be large or small, and whoever you invite to officiate for you, this delightful book will inspire you and guide you in deciding how to make your ceremony personal and meaningful, and help to send you on your way at the end of the ceremony with the happy noise of congratulations ringing in your ears. Your wedding ceremony has the promise and potential to be at the heart of one of the most magical days of your life and it deserves considerable thought. This book will keep you on track, so enjoy the process, and no matter what, have fun as you prepare! Whatever you choose, it's the start of your married life. Congratulations! Go well!

Introduction

I f you are reading this book, then I guess you are planning your wedding ceremony – so, congratulations! Although many of the couples I marry want to have an input into their ceremony and to make it both personal and special, not many people want to actually sit down and create the whole of their ceremony from scratch. This book has been written to help you think through the process of your wedding ceremony, so that you can work with your chosen celebrant to create your perfect ceremony together. The book will give you some ideas and practical help, and will guide you through all the main aspects of a modern wedding.

A few years ago brides and grooms had very little choice about the content of their wedding ceremony – certainly they could choose music, hymns and readings, but the options for these were often constrained, there was little choice about the rest of your ceremony, and almost no choice about the vows and the promises that you made to each other.

I work as a Celebrant, and fortunately things have changed. In the 21st Century, we expect to be able to personalise most things in our lives, from the ringtone on our phones to the way in which we access our bank accounts. Wedding ceremonies are no different. In fact, on a day when the bride and groom are setting out to create the most special of occasions, the wedding ceremony should encompass the most personal of your choices.

Of course, the decisions you make about the type of ceremony you have will impact on what you can include, but most celebrants, officiants, registrars, and ministers that I have spoken to are happy to discuss your ceremony and agree what is appropriate. I am very fortunate – I live and work in Scotland, where the legal process allows me to include all the ideas in this book. So if you have difficulty in agreeing the kind of ceremony you want to have, you could always come to Scotland!

What is so important about a ceremony?

Some couples spend months, even years, planning all the aspects of their wedding – the venue, the food, the colour scheme, the dance music – and then realise that they have given little thought to the actual ceremony. Fortunately, many people consider the ceremony to be the most important part of the day; after all, without it you are simply having a big (and expensive!) party.

For thousands of years, humans have honoured major life transitions through ceremony, ritual, and storytelling. We may feel uncomfortable with the words "ceremony" or "ritual", thinking they are associated with religion and dogmatic practices. Yet we still gather our community of friends and family together when someone graduates, becomes pregnant, or dies. These community events are the same as ceremony, regardless of religion or belief. They create a space for people to be together and to honour the person or event, and secular ceremonies can have as much beauty, substance, meaning, and power as a church ceremony

Ceremonies can be intricate and elaborate, or they can be as simple as lighting a candle and expressing our gratitude or feelings, or making a formal declaration. In ceremonies we give each other recognition and honour, or we express love and devotion, or we mark and honour achievements. And often in a ceremony we incorporate rituals and traditions. Traditions connect us to our past, to our history and ancestry. They are often symbolic of culture and values, and they are an opportunity to link the past to the future, preserving old customs or developing and creating new ones.

Even if you are choosing to have a simple marriage ceremony conducted in a register office or courthouse, there will still be a process and a structure that is being followed. All ceremonies are events which have a ritual significance, and are performed on a special occasion. The theory surrounding ceremony suggests that there are three components to every ceremony – the arrival and preparations (separation from the old state), a point of transition or transformation, and an exit or incorporation into the newly-formed state of identity or community. Whether it is a school graduation, a private and intimate dedication, or an international event, there are similar elements in most ceremonies: a clear purpose; a theatrical component, performance or physical display; maybe a procession, or another way of involving the people who are present; a declaration or verbal pronouncement; and a triumphant ending.

In the UK a few years ago, the Olympic Games in London started with the Opening Ceremony. Whatever you made of it, and the quirkiness that it represented – and despite the millions of people who were watching it across the world – on the following pages we can see similarities between that event and a wedding...

2012 Olympic Opening Ceremony		A Typical Wedding	
Prologue	Music concert to celebrate the national history. Red arrows flypast	Before the wedding starts	Guests arrive and are seated. Maybe the groom is on hand to meet them. Perhaps some music is playing.
Countdown	The formal start of proceedings including the ringing of the Olympic Bell	Entrance	Formal start of the wedding, including arrival music and the entrance of the bridal party.
Setting the Scene	History of 'Green and Pleasant Land'	Welcome and Opening words	Being clear about the purpose of the event
Story	Various dramatic and musical pieces to represent the history of UK and London	Celebrant's Address	Something of your story, and the context in which you are coming to make this commitment.
Involving other people	Parade of athletes	Involving important people	Readings, singing, guests declaration of support Symbolic gestures

Formal proceedings	Sebastian Coe's (Chair of the London Olympics) address	Marriage vows and exchange of rings	Formal words about marriage Marriage Vows
Declaration	The Queen's official opening of the games	Pronouncement	Legal declaration of marriage
Closing section	Lighting the Olympic Cauldron	Closing the ceremony	Signing the legal paperwork Closing words, blessings, or gestures
Finish	Fireworks Rock concert	Recessional	Presentation of the newly-married couple The married couple walk out amidst clapping and cheering and music.

The chapters in this book describe each of the key elements and give you some ideas to think about when planning your own ceremony. You may want to look through everything, or you may want to concentrate on one or two chapters.

What will make MY wedding unique and personal?

After being involved in hundreds of weddings, I can truly say that each one is different. Couples may say the same or similar words, they may get married in the same venue, and even on the same day as another couple, yet such is the individuality of human beings and their relationships that each wedding ceremony feels distinctive and unique. So don't worry if you haven't come up with a grand idea for your wedding, or that you will be somehow copying your friends if you choose to include a similar reading or symbolic gesture. There is no need to hunt for gimmicks to make your big day special. The two of you are bringing yourselves, your expressions of love and commitment to each other, your hopes and dreams for the future – and that is what makes your wedding ceremony unique.

Having said that, the ideas and the words in this book are designed to stimulate your creativity, to help you think through how best to put your feelings about each other into words, and to find the language that best says what you want to express. You don't have to be a poet or a writer to create a beautiful ceremony, you simply have to spend some time (alone, or with each other) exploring ideas and following your heart and your instincts.

Use the book as a way of discussing your plans with the person you are getting married to – write on the pages of the book, highlight words and phrases that you love, score out the things that you hate! Scribble your thoughts in the margins, or use the blank spaces to list ideas or important points. And encourage your partner to do the same.

Oh, and don't forget to have fun and enjoy it!

Jane Patmore

A note about same-sex marriage

When I started writing this book, it was around the time that the law in Scotland was changing to allow same-sex marriage to be legal. It has been a wonderful freedom for me, as a celebrant, to be able to say 'Yes' when a same-sex couple ask if I can hold their legal ceremony. Somewhat naively, I imagined that I could write a book which was equally open to everyone. However, for years I have used different forms of words and questions and examples for same-sex marriage, for vow renewals and for other ceremonies, so I don't know why I imagined that a change in the law would solve all the problems.

The fact is that 'marriage' has its roots in a very gendered system, and also a very patriarchal system. In a world in which we are ceasing to use gendered terms – actor/actress; waiter/waitress; chairman/chairwoman, etc. – the language and symbolism of weddings remains heavily gendered, (unsurprisingly) with special names for bride, groom, husband, wife. This has made it impossible to write a book (or at least a book that is readable) which encompasses all the possible terms and combinations.

It is with some regret that THIS particular book is written for a predominantly heterosexual (cis) readership. However, it is my intention to very quickly write another book containing the same ideas and concepts, but with language more appropriate for same-sex couples, and which also addresses the specific questions and freedoms that arise in same-sex marriage. I look forward to a time when language is sufficiently neutral to be all-inclusive.

Chapter 1: The Arrival

'Please stand for the entrance of the bridal party.'

It's the moment we've all been waiting for. The bride senses that excited flutter when the music starts up, the doors open, and she takes her first steps down the aisle. Guests turn and strive to catch their initial glimpse of the bride. The groom turns to meet her eyes as she walks towards him. Perhaps the bride's father is walking proudly beside his daughter, or the couple's children are dancing with excitement…

It sounds so simple. And yet creating that perfect moment is not quite so easy – there's the choice of music, deciding the order of the bridal party as they arrive, and all the arrangements that have been made in the ceremony room or space before the wedding begins.

Terry and Amy had planned a lovely ceremony. They had written their own vows and had chosen lots of personal touches. Terry clearly adored Amy, and was willing to do anything she wanted so that she could have her perfect day. However, during their planning, Amy was the one who had understood all the detail of what was happening – where the guests would sit, how the room should be set out. Terry had no disagreement about what she was suggesting, but unfortunately he didn't have the focus on detail that Amy had. Half an hour before the ceremony started, Terry was in a panic. He knew that special candles had been bought, but he didn't know where they were. He wasn't sure whether there were enough copies of the Order of Service for guests to have one each, and he had forgotten which family members were to sit in the front two rows.

Of course, everything was sorted before Amy arrived, but it probably wasn't the relaxed start that Terry had been looking forward to. So here is my first piece of advice: Remember that the bridal party will be the last to arrive for the ceremony, so it is important that whatever plans are agreed are known and understood by whoever will be at the venue before the bride. This may be the ushers, the wedding planner, the co-ordinator at your wedding venue, your celebrant, the groom, or even another guest. But make sure that people know who is responsible, and preferably have important instructions written down.

Traditions

In making the preparations, there are traditions that you can follow to help you, or you can choose to do your own thing.

Often the ushers or groomsmen are the first to arrive at the venue, at least thirty minutes before the ceremony starts. They should be informed in advance of how to seat the guests as they arrive. Even if your ceremony is relaxed and informal, your guests may be concerned about sitting in the 'wrong' seat, and I often notice how reluctant people are to sit in the rows near to the front. It can be a good idea to have place names for the important seats – the closest family, for example – and to mark which rows are reserved for named individuals. It always helps if the ushers know who the guests are, and can recognise them, to prevent a much loved aunt from taking a seat quietly near the back of the room while there is a vacant seat for her in the second row.

In most Western weddings, the front right-hand row of seats (or the first couple of rows) are reserved for the groom's closest family, and the front left-hand row of seats is reserved for the bride's closest family. That is the right and left sides as you enter from the back of the room, not looking from the front. The number of rows you need to reserve will depend on the size of your families, and your plans for whether the bride and groom's attendants will sit or stand (more on that in a moment).

If your wedding is very formal, you may have a seating plan for all guests at the ceremony. But more often, once close family are seated, other guests can choose their place. Some couples have adopted the approach that 'Today two families become one – so pick a seat, not a side', and an internet search will bring up some lovely creative examples of notices and signs that people have made. Having this kind of flexibility is particularly important if there is disparity in the size of your families – where one partner has a small close family, and the other has endless uncles and cousins – or if you have lots of guests who are joint friends of you both.

Of course, not all families have harmonious relationships. Sometimes parents are separated, divorced, or have new partners, and it takes some care to be sensitive to everyone's feelings about where various members of an extended family should sit during the ceremony. This is easier to manage if it is an informal wedding, and I have seen many and various options to help smooth things through. One bride had recently separated parents whose relationship was acrimonious, and she placed her parents at either end of the front row with three bridesmaids in between – with her sister sitting in the middle, so that she was not seen to be taking side with either Mum or Dad!

If you are planning to involve guests in your ceremony, perhaps giving a reading or in some other way, then make sure that these people can get out of their seat easily, and are preferably sitting next to an aisle.

It may also be worth giving some thought to any guests who are less mobile – maybe allowing room for a wheel-chair, or if you have guests with infants they may need space for a buggy/stroller or baby seat. Young children attending a wedding is a much debated topic, and often guests with toddlers or young children may prefer to sit near the back or somewhere that they can get out easily if the child becomes upset.

Preparation of the Ceremony Venue or Space

Some brides have a strong mental image of how the room will look as they arrive at their wedding, perhaps filled with the colour and scent of flowers, decorated with a red carpet or following a particular colour theme, or with the aisle lit with romantic candles. I have seen some wonderful alternatives, too. For example, an autumn wedding where the aisle was strewn with autumn leaves rather than petals, or a room decorated with brightly coloured helium-filled balloons and bunting.

If you plan to use candles, I'd like to offer a word of warning. I have witnessed several heart-stopping moments when a bride has swept down the aisle and, in the process, her dress has brushed over the tops of candle flames. I've also had to step in on one occasion when a guest was standing chatting, oblivious to the fact that her dress was hovering above a flame and was starting to smoulder. So, despite the amazing effect that candlelight can bring, please think carefully about how they will be used safely.

The Bridal Party

In the majority of weddings that I have held, the groom arrives at the ceremony venue with his best man and groomsmen about half an hour before the wedding. This gives him time to attend to any last minute details or arrangements, and also allows plenty of time for your photographer to take some shots of the men – especially those jokey photos of the groom looking worried and his groomsmen looking at their watches, or the best man trying to hold the groom back as he pretends to escape. But, more seriously, it provides time for some lovely photos of the groom's family – him with his mum and dad, or other family members.

Although most wedding arrivals follow this format, it is also becoming more common for the bride and the groom to enter the ceremony together. For some couples, it feels less nerve-racking; for others, it reflects a more modern approach to the start of marriage – the two of you approaching it together, equal and side-by-side.

Often the next to arrive at the venue are the bridesmaids and the mother of the bride, although the bride's mother may come in advance on her own. Usually the bride's mother waits at the entrance of the venue until the bride arrives – it may be the first time she has seen her daughter in her wedding dress – and then, when the bridal party are almost ready, the bride's mother enters the ceremony room. Some people prefer to slip in quietly with a minimum of fuss, and others choose to make a more formal entrance, maybe with music, and perhaps accompanied by an usher or groomsman who shows her to her seat. The arrival of the bride's mother is a signal to the groom that his bride has arrived, but it is amazing how long it takes for those last minute adjustments to the dress, or a final few photos, and those moments can feel like a loooong time for the waiting groom.

So now, at last, we are ready for the music to start and your guests to stand for the arrival of the Bride ☺

In traditional weddings, the bridesmaids would take their places behind the bride. This works well in a grand space such as a church or cathedral, where there is a long aisle and plenty of room at the front for the bridesmaids to follow the bride and still have enough room to get to their places. It also reflects one of the traditional jobs of the bridesmaid – arranging the train of the wedding dress or the veil. You can see this in photos of the marriage of Catherine Middleton to Prince William. However, not many people get married in such a location, or have a train which is more than nine feet long. And not many people are getting married to a future king!

Most wedding venues have substantially less space, and it has become more normal practice for the flower-girls and bridesmaids to enter first. Depending on the space, the music you have chosen and the temperament of your bridesmaids, they may want to enter in pairs or they may arrive one by one. The bridesmaids enter and stand on the left, awaiting the arrival of the bride.

When Debbie was marrying Malcolm, neither of her parents were at her wedding – her mum had died many years earlier and her father was not much involved in her life. Debbie couldn't think of another relative who she was really close to, and she made her entrance accompanied by her seven-year-old son, Liam. As Debbie and Liam walked down the aisle, Malcolm walked up the aisle to meet them halfway, and the three of them walked to the front together.

Often the bride is accompanied by her father, but this is not always possible, or sometimes there may be other choices to make. Brides arrive with their mother, an uncle, a brother, a step-parent, their children (be they adults or small children), with more than one person, or on their own. Whoever is accompanying the bride, it is often simplest if they are on the bride's left as she walks. This means that when they get to the front, the bride will arrive with the groom next to her on her right. The person accompanying the bride can then simply step away to the left to get to their seat, without any complex movements of having to step behind the bride and avoid treading on her dress.

Of course it is always nice to express whatever comes naturally at that point – a kiss for the bride, a hug, or a handshake for the groom.

'Giving Away' the Bride

In the most traditional forms of wedding, it would be customary for the Celebrant to ask: 'Who gives this woman to be married to this man?' to which the response would be: 'I do.' Some view this to have its roots in antiquated or sexist tradition, while others are happy to accept it as a way for a father, or other important person, to show their support for the marriage. Whatever your opinion on this, there are alternative words which can be used to demonstrate appreciation for your parents, or for them to demonstrate their blessing for your marriage. For example:

Celebrant/Officiant: Who supports Amanda in her marriage to John?

Amanda's Dad: I do.

OR

Celebrant/Officiant: Who support Amanda and John in their marriage?

Amanda's parents and John's parents (together): We do.

OR

Celebrant/Officiant: Who presents this couple to be married?

Amanda's parents and John's parents (together): We do.

OR

Celebrant/Officiant: Who has guided these people through life, nurtured and loved them, encouraged their independence?

Parents stand

Celebrant/Officiant: Who supports them as they join in marriage?

Amanda's parents and John's parents (together): We do.

I conducted one wedding where the bride insisted I should ask the most traditional of questions – and so I did: 'Who brings this woman to be married to this man?' To which the bride answered: 'I bring myself, but with the blessing and support of my family.' ☺

And, of course, it is enough for the accompanying person simply to walk the bride to the end of the aisle and then to sit without saying anything.

In most weddings that I hold, if the bride has a veil, she wears it back rather than over her face. However, if the bride arrives with her face covered, then you need to decide at what point it is taken back, and who will do that – the bride herself, her father, the groom, or one of her attendants? From a very practical point of view, you need someone who is tall enough to reach over the bride's head, and someone with enough sensitivity to manage that without messing up her hair!

To sit or to stand?

Once the bridal party have arrived at the front of the room – what then? Do the bridesmaids and groomsmen sit or stand, and what about the bride and groom – do they stand with their backs to their guests, or face each other? Do they get a chance to sit?

First things first. I always encourage a couple to greet each other in whatever way feels right and natural to them. Often the groom and bride will not have seen each other that day. The bride arrives next to her groom looking amazing and wearing a dress he may never have seen, and both of you are full of excited anticipation. For a long time, probably for years, the two of you will have been together for most of life's big events and emotional moments. Yet the hours before your wedding have been spent apart. So when you see each other, you should hug, kiss, blink away a tear or two, smile, laugh, whisper a few words to each other, hold hands – whatever is going to make you feel relaxed and happy and loved.

Most often, I suggest that the bride and groom turn to face each other. This means that the guests see a bit more than the backs of your heads, and it also means that the bridesmaids can help with sorting out the train or veil – no point in having a beautiful dress and not showing it off to best effect. Another alternative is for the bride and groom to face their guests, although some couples find the thought of this makes them too nervous.

At the start of the ceremony, it is nice for the brides-maids and best man/groomsmen to remain standing in support of the couple, then once the words of introduc-tion are over, for them to either sit down, or to step back slightly. This can signal a change in the tempo of the ceremony, from the section which is about cheerfully welcoming everyone to the rest of the ceremony, which then starts to turn its focus to the couple getting married. It is also worth considering the position of your attendants vis-à-vis your photographer. If there is limited space for you all to stand, then seating the bridesmaids and best man/groomsmen leaves clear space for photos unobscured by the back of the best man's head.

An emotional moment?

Well, of course it is, and that is good. You're making a big commitment to the person you love and you're there surrounded by your closest friends and family; they are supporting you, and wishing you everything good for your marriage. The point at which the bride makes her entrance is charged with emotion for the bride, the groom, and for many of your guests. So what can you do to keep your emotions under control? How can you avoid the feeling that these emotions might overwhelm you?

The best thing you can do to manage your feelings is to prepare – prepare yourself so that your emotions build gradually and are manageable. Three things can help with this:

1. **Visualisation** – imagine what it is going to be like as you take those first steps down the aisle, or as you turn to see your bride walk towards you. Don't try to push the emotion away, but try out different techniques to help reduce your emotions if they are threatening to overcome you. Perhaps practise some breathing exercises, or have

something physical to hold as a reminder of calm reality, or repeat a calming mantra in your mind. Practise using these in the weeks before your wedding whenever a stressful moment occurs.

2. **Practise** – say your vows out loud, lock yourself away in a quiet place and speak them clearly, slowly and loudly – your mouth and tongue will become accustomed to the words and their sequence.

3. **Ask your celebrant about a rehearsal,** - if you are anxious. You might feel more confident if you have walked through the ceremony and know where you will stand and when you will have to move.

Some couples find that the idea of the bride walking down the aisle to meet the groom is just too nerve-racking, and they choose to meet in a more private moment before the ceremony and make their entrance together. Remember, at the end of the day, everyone who is there is an invited guest – your family and your closest friends – and they are all there because they are happy for you. You may be surprised by how delightful it is to walk in and see everyone you love smiling at your arrival. And a few happy tears or an emotional giggle is all part of the excitement.

Just a few close friends...

Even if you are having a tiny wedding with very few guests, and you don't need elaborate seating plans, think about the details beforehand – and make sure that someone knows what you want, so that your arrival to the space is relaxed and right.

What do YOU want?

- Who is in your bridal party? What order will they arrive in?

- Do you need a seating plan for the first couple of rows?

- How will the ceremony space be prepared or decorated?

- Where will you stand for the ceremony? Will you sit during any of it?

- Who can you trust to make sure everything is going smoothly on the day?

Chapter 2: Welcome and Opening Words

I f you are creating a personal ceremony, it is important that right from the start, from the very first words which are spoken, this celebration is about YOU. This is the opportunity to set the scene for your ceremony, and often for the rest of your day. So what kind of tone or mood do you want to create? Is your wedding to be relaxed and informal? Does it have a theme? Perhaps there is a focus on family all being together, or maybe you are hoping to create a dream fairy-tale event. Sometimes the setting or venue for your ceremony will influence the mood, and a wedding in an ancient historic castle will have a very different feel to a wedding outside in a garden or on a beach.

Maybe there is something significant about the location – the beach where the groom proposed; the city where you both went to college; a favourite place from your childhood; the venue where your parents were married. All of these little details add to the personalisation of your ceremony, and whether you want them mentioned explicitly, or not, let your celebrant know if there is something like this which influenced your choice of venue.

It may be similar with the date for your wedding. Is it an anniversary, or a favourite time of year? Maybe you chose it because it is the week after the groom's birthday and it makes it more likely that he will remember the anniversary. ☺

Sometimes a good place to start is by picking out the words which best sum up what you hope your ceremony will be like. This list might give you some ideas to start with:

Traditional	Light-hearted	Funny
Relaxed	Romantic	Family-focussed Party
Private	Intimate	Nature
Woodland	Quirky	Blend of cultures
Fairy-tale	Beach-themed	Celtic
Seasonal	Mystical	Sci-Fi
Serious	Contemporary	

Pick out a few which feel important to you, or add your own, and use those ideas to create opening words which pick up on the themes. You can do this yourself, or you can tell your celebrant which concepts you want to reflect and they can create the opening paragraphs for you. For example:

'We have gathered today in this wonderful historic location to celebrate the marriage of Keith and Katie. Their wedding honours the most ancient of traditions and blends them with contemporary words, creating a ceremony which reflects the unique qualities which Katie and Keith have blended in their relationship. It incorporates Keith's work as an art historian, and Katie's passion for poetry.'

OR

*'This afternoon we celebrate as Alistair and Berihan
are married and their children become part of one
family. We welcome all the children who are here, and
hope that everyone enjoys the relaxed ceremony and
the opportunity to spend a day with family and close
friends, to laugh, to play, to dance and to sing.'*

It is often effective to use a short quotation if you can
find one that is relevant – maybe a few lines of poetry,
or words from a song, or a quote from a favourite film
or book. If you can't find anything you think is suitable,
ask your celebrant or officiant to help you find something.
They will have access to lots of resources, and will be able
to give you examples to look at. If you are creating your
own ceremony, the internet is an amazing tool for finding
quotes. Search online for 'quote' and 'love' and then whatever word is important to you – this can help you to find
some incredible quotations.

*Tad and Ellie love to be outdoors. They run, hike, cycle,
and walk their dog on the beach. Their wedding took place
on a beach and really close to a spectacular mountain. The
ceremony included words written by Anne Morrow Lindberg
reflecting that relationships are like islands washed by the
ebb and flow of the changing tides, and they also used this
beautiful quotation from the naturalist John Muir: 'Climb
the mountains and get their good tidings. Nature's peace
will flow into you as sunshine flows into trees. The winds
will blow their own freshness into you, and the storms their
energy, while cares will drop away from you like the leaves
of Autumn.'*

Why are we here?

As well as setting the mood, the opening words are the point at which we make the purpose of the event clear. I know that sounds a bit obvious – after all, you have invited your guests to your wedding, and there you are standing in front of them waiting to be married – but part of the scene-setting is to clarify what you are expecting from yourself or your guests. For example:

'As Ann and Walter join in marriage, we are here to witness their vows, show them our support, offer them encouragement, share in their happiness, participate in their blessing, honour their relationship and celebrate their love.'

OR

'Walter and Ann are here today to make their promises to one another, share their dreams, build their future, to express their love, and to seek your support for their marriage as they embark on a new adventure in life.'

Sometimes a marriage ceremony includes other specific purposes, too. It may honour the marriages of parents, include a baby naming or blessing, or celebrate the creation of a blended family. When I held the wedding for Nancy and Alexander, the ceremony was held in the garden of their new home so we included a house blessing in their service, using words which reflected hospitality, welcoming, security, stability, and warmth.

Can you write three or four sentences to describe what is important about your wedding ceremony? This list of phrases may give you some ideas, or you can add your own....

The Couple Getting Married	Their Guests
Proclaim your love	Participate in a joyful occasion
Accept each other as lifelong partners	Celebrate one of life's greatest moments
Commit to support one another in love	Acknowledge the love of the couple
Celebrate your relationship and friendship	Witness the promises that will be made
Share the occasion with your closest family	Support the couple as they make their commitment
Affirm your devotion and commitment	Share in a wonderful celebration
Unite you in marriage	Encourage them in their new adventure
Make your promises to each other	Bless the couple in their dreams for the future
Welcome your family and friends	Delight in their happiness

Welcome one and all

In addition to a general welcome to your guests, it can be nice to show your appreciation that friends and family have made the effort to join you. People may have taken time away from work, cut short vacations, or travelled long distances to be with you at your wedding. You may want to do this in general terms by acknowledging and thanking everyone, or you may want to make specific mention of people who have travelled a long way, and even where they have come from.

When Guan-Yin and Joey were married, they had guests from across the world but they wanted to show their appreciation for everyone who was there: 'Joey and Guan-yin are delighted that so many friends and family members could join them today – family from China, who are taking this opportunity for a holiday; friends and colleagues who have travelled from New Zealand, South Africa and Bermuda; and those from closer by, who have set aside their routines and commitments to be here and celebrate with us this afternoon. Welcome to you all.'

Of course, it is not always possible for everyone that you love to be with you at your wedding. Maybe you have friends and family who live too far away and cannot travel, or some who may be elderly or unwell, or maybe you are having a small ceremony and it has not been possible to invite everyone who would like to be there. It is a nice touch to mention those who may be thinking about you on your special day, wishing you well, toasting your future, or maybe those with whom you will celebrate at a later time.

Sometimes a family has been affected by loss, and those you have loved and who have been close to you have died. There are many ways in which we can remember people and acknowledge the importance of their presence in our lives. Some of these are silent, maybe unseen and known only to the couple – for example, the inclusion of a brooch in the bride's bouquet, or the use of a particular colour which had been a grandmother's favourite. It may feel appropriate to have something to represent those whose lives have passed, maybe a photo or a candle. And sometimes people want to make a specific acknowledgement during the ceremony, either by directly mentioning the person's name or with a more oblique reference, acknowledging those who have been important in your life and who are in your hearts and thoughts on the day of your wedding.

Although this sounds like something sad on an otherwise happy day, it is important for some couples to acknowledge their loss, perhaps to appreciate their sense that their loved one is somehow present, or to accept that life has many ups and downs and that during those difficult moments in life the support of your partner or spouse is of particular comfort. Your celebrant will know how to include something like this in a sensitive way and at an appropriate point, so that it doesn't change the mood of the occasion.

Religious or not religious, or something else?

Depending on where in the world you are getting married, and the type of ceremony you have chosen, you may not have much choice of whether your ceremony is inclusive of your beliefs and those of your family and friends. Some church weddings may require you to follow a set liturgy, and some civil ceremonies may not permit you to include religious or spiritual words or music.

I am fortunate, living and working in Scotland, as I can hold a ceremony which is flexible and can include whatever is important and meaningful to the couple getting married, and which can also reflect traditions of the wider circle of family and friends.

Speak with the celebrant or officiant who is conducting your wedding, and find out what they can permit. However, more importantly, discuss it with the person you are getting married to, and set out your own ideals. It may be straightforward and you might both share the same belief or faith, or you could be in complete agreement that you want to have a non-religious or secular ceremony. I know from my experience, however, that it is not always so easy. Perhaps you want a secular ceremony but it is important for a family member that a prayer is included, or maybe you and your partner hold different beliefs. Or possibly you find it very difficult to describe what you feel. Maybe you have a perception of something spiritual or a deep connection with nature. Perhaps you have a sense of something that you cannot easily define. Is it possible to include that in your ceremony?

My own training and the legislation in Scotland gives me great flexibility, and here are some of the ways in which I have included different beliefs and opinions:

(I recognise that those who have a strong belief would want to get married within their own faith community, and what I suggest here does not attempt or pretend to represent any other faith or belief system.)

Scenario

The couple getting married do not go to church and would feel uncomfortable about going to church just for their wedding, but they each retain a belief in God and would like that included in their wedding ceremony.

Options

Name the belief that the couple hold: 'We are here today in the presence of the God of Love.'

Include a prayer that the couple have chosen, or that the celebrant has suggested.

Include readings from texts or sacred books that have meaning for the couple.

Make specific reference to the couple's belief in their vows and rings exchange: 'In the presence of a loving God, do you, Anton, accept Claire as your wife?' or 'You ask that these rings are blessed and are a constant reminder of your love for each other and the Divine love which supports you.'

Scenario

The couple come from different faith backgrounds. Neither person adheres to their religion strongly, but they each want something of their tradition included in the wedding.

Options

Be clear in the opening words what the ceremony is setting out to do, and acknowledge differences in practice and ritual: 'For Abbas and Lucy, it is important that their ceremony honours the different beliefs that they hold and respects the traditions in which they were raised. Lucy and Abbas have invited family members to read from sacred texts and to sing, and I know that they have both enjoyed participating in traditional wedding preparations over the last few days.'

Invite family members from each faith to contribute.

Explain the meaning and metaphor behind any symbolic gestures, and try to be as inclusive as possible to all your guests.

Scenario

The couple hold different beliefs.

Options

Acknowledge the differences: 'We all know that Brian is a scientist and a determined follower of logic and rationality, whilst Angela follows a path which delights in angels and everlasting souls. Today their marriage is a unique blend of the practical and the magical, a celebration of legal commitment and the mystery of love and life. So be amazed by our world of atoms and electrons which create our physical reality, and the neurochemicals which control and stimulate our emotions, and yet also allow yourself to wonder at the unseen forces which draw two people together into a bond of love with each other and trust in the mystery of an unknown future...'

Scenario

The couple do not follow any religion and would prefer a secular ceremony, however the groom's family all have a strong faith and he does not want to upset them by ignoring it.

Options

Welcome guests of all faiths and beliefs, and explain that it is important to the couple getting married that everyone feels welcomed and accepted, and that their good wishes, thoughts of love, blessings or prayers are appreciated equally.

Use a wedding blessing which has a prayerful tone without being religious: 'May the road rise to meet you, may the wind be always on your back, may the sun shine warm upon your face, may pure be the joy that surrounds you, may true be the hearts that love you.'

When Emma and Steve were married, they chose a non-religious ceremony. However, a much loved aunt was an ordained minister and it meant a lot to her to be able to come forward and bless the couple, offering a prayer for them in line with her own strongly held beliefs.

Scenario

The couple are not religious but they feel they are spiritual.

Options

Use phrases which are meaningful to the couple's beliefs: 'May the spirit of love be always in your lives.' 'Above you are the stars and below you is the earth. Like the stars, your love should be a constant source of light, and like the earth, a firm foundation from which to grow.'

There may be a particular place or theme or action which reflects the spiritual connection, e.g. light and the space of the sky; or nature and water; or healing touch. When Jamila and Zak were married, they included a gesture where each of them – after their vows – touched their chest above their heart, then touched the chest of their partner, expressing the heart connection that they recognised between the two of them.

What is important to YOU?

- What is most important about your ceremony? Is there a feeling or mood that you want to capture?

- Are there lines from songs, or words from a film or book, which sum up how you feel about each other?

- Where have your guests travelled from? Do you want to make any special mentions of people or places? Are there loved ones who can't be with you? If your families will be present, is there anything that it would be helpful for your celebrant to be aware of, either within your families, or between your families?

- Do either of you have children (if so, what are their names and ages)? Will they attend the wedding? Would you like them to be involved in the ceremony in any way?

YOUR BELIEFS

In our modern multicultural world, your wedding is likely to include guests who hold a wide range of faiths and beliefs – some based on religious precepts; some on traditions and cultural influences; and some derived from science and rational thought. The following questions help to set out which of these, if any, are important for you to include in your ceremony.

- Is there a belief system that is important to either of you? Are you religious, non-religious, humanist, spiritual, or not sure? Do you want anything of those beliefs reflected in your ceremony? Do you have a space or environment when you feel most 'connected' or at peace – for example, in nature, or while dancing?

- Would you like to include a prayer or a non-religious blessing or prayerful thoughts during your ceremony? Are there terms such as God, love, Divine presence, spirit of love, Angels, universal connection, shared humanity, eternal love, etc. which are meaningful for you, or which you would prefer to avoid?

- If you do not want a prayer or blessing, would you like an opportunity for people to be still and quiet, to collect their thoughts and to focus on you/marriage/the meaning of love? Or to (silently) offer their thoughts of love, good wishes, and blessing for your future?

- Is there a dominant belief system held by the majority of your family and friends attending the wedding? Is it different from your own? Is it important to have an acknowledgement of the variety of faiths and beliefs?

Chapter 3: Your Story

I often ask couples about wedding ceremonies at which they have been guests, and what they liked (or didn't like) about them. The vast majority of people reply that it is the degree to which the ceremony feels personal and meaningful. A personal ceremony is an opportunity to state the intention, purpose, and vision for your marriage, and surround it with power and love. It should be an authentic reflection of who you are as a couple, and as individuals, and where you are heading together.

I hold many weddings, and it is a wonderful role to have in life. At its heart, a wedding ceremony is a celebration of the relationship of each individual couple; and no two relationships are the same. The way each person feels about their relationship, the way that they speak about it, or express it to each other and the world, varies enormously – and this is what makes each ceremony unique and special.

The weddings I hold are in a variety of places and locations. So it was very unusual, towards the end of 2014, when I looked at my diary and saw that I had three consecutive weddings in the same venue. The first thing I did was to panic slightly in case I had mis-transcribed some information, but after checking my records it turned out that, yes, three weddings were in the same venue.

For me, this occurrence reinforced how completely different each wedding is. Even in the same season, at the same venue, and with the same venue team co-ordinating and supporting the event, each of those three ceremonies was unique: different in the readings and music chosen; different in the vows and promises they made; but also different because each of them reflected the couple getting married – who they were as individuals and as a couple, and also something of their story and journey together.

Of course, there are words which are heard frequently during a ceremony – love, trust, commitment, and so on – but what really brings a ceremony to life is how those emotions and values have played out in the couple's relationship so far, and what they both hope those words will mean to them in the future.

Hazel and Gordon met in Hong Kong, and what started as a holiday romance developed and endured. Hazel lived in California and Gordon lived in Scotland, and for three years they had a long distance relationship until Hazel relocated to Scotland. For Gordon and Hazel, COMMITMENT to their relationship meant that each of them made the effort to carve out time and money to visit each other. It meant the commitment to rearranging free-time and being available late night or early morning, so they could speak on Skype when they were on different continents and in different time zones. For their future they were making a commitment to be together wherever life took them – and at the time of their marriage they were not certain whether their jobs and home would be in the US or the UK, but their commitment was that it would always be together.

For Helen and Kit, COMMITMENT took on a very different hue. When Kit and Helen met, Helen had a young daughter, Amy. A few months into their relationship, it became apparent that Amy had a genetic condition which seriously limited her ability and her life. Facing such pressure, some relationships would go under, but such was Kit's commitment that he determined to stand by Helen and Amy, and support them no matter what. At times, Amy's illness left Helen exhausted and overwhelmed, but she had made the commitment to share her life with Kit and so she always made arrangements to ensure that there was time when she and Kit could have space on their own to be a couple. In the near future, when Amy's life draws to a close, Helen and Kit have committed to be there for each other through the difficult process, to support each other. And as time passes and their anguish softens, they have made a commitment to help each other find some new happiness in life.

Two relationships and marriages based on commitment, but coming from the heart of two very different stories.

How Much Detail?

For some couples, it feels important that their wedding ceremony includes the whole story of their time together – how they met, how their friendship and relationship developed, the ups (and downs), the adventures, events, and humorous occasions that they have shared. This may seem like a lot, and is certainly too much for some couples. But sometimes the way in which two people cope with the curve ball events that life throws at them illuminates how they really work as a team, how they support each other in good times and bad, help to change a bad mood to a better one, to deal with setbacks, or to share good news and excitement.

Even if you don't intend to share much of the detail of your life story during your ceremony, I would encourage you to tell your celebrant or officiant as much as you feel comfortable with. I have had couples tell me things which are sad, or secret, or not talked about within their family, or tell me ridiculous and hilarious stories which are definitely not for re-telling with elderly aunts amongst the guests! But all of these help me to understand the mood of the ceremony and the relationship.

At the end of this chapter, there are some questions about your own story. Whether you are planning to share a lot or a little, and whether you are writing the ceremony with a celebrant or on your own, these questions can be really helpful. Answer them separately, and compare notes or discuss them together. Write down whatever feels important, and then summarise it if you don't want all the detail included.

As an example, in Helen and Kit's wedding (see box text above), they didn't want to dwell on Amy's illness, and the phrases used in the ceremony were: *'For Kit and Helen, being together and getting married is all about commitment: to each other, to their family, and to their future – being open to love and happiness, and to the continued exploration of a new chapter of life together.'* The phrases weren't complicated or explicit, but when you know a little of Helen and Kit's story, you can sense the richness contained in those few words.

'Please – Nothing Soppy!'

You would be surprised (or maybe not) by how often couples – and particularly the groom – cringe at the idea that their wedding ceremony will include some words describing how the couple feel about each other. This is especially true in my native Scotland, where people are known for their ability to chat to anyone and everyone at a bus stop, but clam up completely if they are asked to talk about their feelings. And yet, when couples take time to sit down and think about what is important about their relationship and what getting married and being together means to them, even the most cynical and reticent partner can come up with some heart-felt words. The words don't have to be eloquent or fancy, and some of the most moving and touching ceremonies are those where the couple have written what they feel very simply in a few words.

So go ahead and try answering some of the questions at the end of this chapter. You might want to do it together, possibly over a glass of wine, or you might want to think about your answers separately and compare notes later. Some couples answer the questions individually and send them to me, and I then work their responses into the ceremony for them both to enjoy, either together when they read the ceremony script for the first time, or as a surprise on the wedding day itself.

Rosalynd and James met at college when they were 16 and 17 years old. They were both part of a large group of classmates who hung around together, and James and Rosalynd become friends gradually, eventually getting together as a couple two years after they first met. They had moved into an apartment together and, although they loved being together and were clearly serious about their care for each other, they often spent time with their larger group of friends. When they were all together, James and Rosalynd were just part of the crowd, never holding hands or being soppy, and it would have been uncomfortable for them to be suddenly declaring their private emotions with their college friends present at their wedding. So they chose to share their sentiments in a less public forum.

This is what was said during their wedding:

'For some couples, getting married is an opportunity to speak about their love for each other and to share funny or romantic stories with all their guests. However, James and Rosalynd are very private people, and it wouldn't feel like THEIR wedding if their deepest feelings were part of this public commitment. However, I have been in a very privileged position – I asked Rosalynd and James some questions about their love for each other, and what being together and getting married means to them, and they decided that the best way for them to do this would be for each of them to write a short piece, which they emailed to me. I can honestly say I have never been so moved by anyone's expression of love, and care, and trust.

I understand that James and Rosalynd have not yet shared their words with each other, but they plan to do so while they are on honeymoon. All I can say is that I believe you have a beautiful future ahead of you. Enjoy.'

Describing YOUR story

There are many books about marriage, and countless poems and songs and films written about love, but sometimes the most meaningful words are those that two people in love say about each other. The following questions guide you through the process of reflecting on what is important and meaningful for you. Don't worry about trying to find the 'perfect' words – your job is to work on the content and the ideas, and it is the role of your celebrant to put that into a format that flows, which reflects your personalities, and which respects your privacy.

Despite the potential for us all to be cynical about love, relationships, and marriage, there is something wonderful about the deep attraction between a couple that has made them decide to take this step. Eventually, there comes a time when a couple consider how much they hope and dream of as their love develops, and how much they are willing to risk to be together and commit to that. In liberal societies, there is not the same pressure as there used to be to get married before setting up a home together, and many people in committed and stable relationships have children before they are married. So it is helpful for you to reflect on what has drawn you to your partner, what has cemented your relationship, and what has moved you to take this step…

Doing this really gives your officiant or celebrant a perspective and insight into the love and connection between you. It can be particularly useful to outline significant challenges that you have faced or overcome – you may not want to have any explicit, or even implicit, reference to this during your ceremony, but it does help your celebrant to understand the background and to celebrate what you have achieved together. And don't forget to tell your celebrant about any other significant events in your life. You might be surprised how often people forget to tell me that they have children, or the importance of animals in their life, or shared interests or careers.

The following simple questions are offered to help you make your preparations for the commitment of marriage in your own way, with as much time and thought as you feel is needed. Please use them as a guideline – they're not intended to be overwhelming. Discuss them and show them to your celebrant. It's their role to gather information from you in order to create the most perfect ceremony for you. And to make a ceremony personal and meaningful, they need some personal background and to find out what is important for you.

ABOUT YOU AND YOUR PARTNER

- How, when, and where did you meet? What attracted you to each other? When did you first feel that you were in love?

- How did your relationship strengthen and develop? What can you say about how it's been since you got together up until now? What are the best things that have happened? Any amusing incidents? Have there been challenges during your time together?

- What do you love, appreciate, and admire most about each other? What is the most important aspect of the relationship, for each of you? What are the three best things about your partner? These can be funny or serious; they don't have to be complex.

Guy and Elena each told me the three things they loved best, but they kept that part secret from each other until the ceremony. Elena says of Guy – he's the kindest person she could meet; full of compassion; she couldn't imagine anyone better. And Guy says, 'Elena makes me complete; she makes me a whole person; and I'd be lost without her.'

THE DECISION TO GET MARRIED

- What does it mean to you both to be getting married? Why is it important to you?

- When/where did you get engaged (if you did)? Was it a surprise or a joint decision? Do you have a proposal story?

- What is important about the ceremony?

- What strengths and qualities are each of you bringing to the marriage? Are there challenges to overcome?

YOUR FUTURE MARRIED LIFE

- How do you hope your future married life together
  will be? Will anything change, or are there things
  that you hope will never change? Do you have any
  specific plans?

- What assumptions are you making about your life
  together: fidelity, family responsibilities, work, where
  you will live, etc? What are you hoping for together?

YOUR SHARED and INDIVIDUAL VALUES

- Which values would you like to base your married life on? What are the fundamental issues which underpin your relationship? List three values each, and give your definitions of what you personally mean by them (they could be the same).

- Is there anything else you'd like your celebrant to know?

Chapter 4: Vows and Promises

Now we are getting down to the nitty-gritty, the real heart of the ceremony. This is the part where you make your legal declarations and your promises to each other. Choosing your vows is an important time. It is an opportunity for you both to think about what you want to say to each other, and which words feel appropriate and right for you for the most personal and intimate part of your ceremony.

For some couples, writing their own vows is what makes the ceremony truly personal – choosing the perfect combination of words to express your love, your aspirations for your relationship, and your commitment to each other. It can seem daunting, but in fact it can be a lovely time for the two of you to focus, before your wedding, on what your marriage is really all about when the dress and the cake and the dance are out of the way.

For other couples, there is something timeless and romantic in using traditional vows. Several people have remarked to me that they just wouldn't feel married if they weren't saying the familiar words they had heard throughout their lives, observed during other people's weddings, or watched in countless films. And even if you are choosing traditional vows, sometimes changing a word here or there can be enough to make them feel like they are truly yours.

However, the MOST important thing is to check what you have to say legally – there is no point in having the most beautifully scripted vows if they do not meet what is required for your particular ceremony. Your requirements may be legal, or they may be related to the type of ceremony you have chosen to have. If you want to make personal vows to each other, check with your celebrant about what is required and what is permitted.

The following pages offer some ideas for you to think about. I suggest that you use them to pick out words or phrases which resonate with you, and to think about how you might want to put them together.

Style and Approach

Often couples want to keep their actual vows brief and simple – anything too private or sentimental might feel embarrassing or awkward, especially in front of family and friends. This really is one of those moments when you are making the most private of statements in the most public of places.

Occasionally, people like their vows to be spontaneous and heart-felt in the moment. This can be very moving, but it is also quite high risk, and I'd suggest that you always have at least a few words written down, in case the emotion of the day gets too much. It is also a good idea for you both to speak with your celebrant about what you think you might say – if only to avoid the scenario where one partner says two brief lines, and the other partner is reading four pages of closely written script!

Have a look at the structure of traditional vows. They often follow a pattern which starts with a question from your celebrant or officiant: 'Do you, Mike, take Clarice to be your wife?' OR 'Are you ready to make the declarations which will join you in marriage?'

Of course the answer is: 'yes' or 'I do'. ☺

This is often followed by the couple making their own statements, which includes some or all of the following:

The context: In the presence of God/With my family and friends as my witnesses/Today surrounded by the love of my family/In the sight of the sea and the sky/Blessed with the presence of Angels/In this special place...

Declaration: I, Nicole, choose you, Fabien, to be my husband/I, Henry, commit myself to you, Adele, in love and marriage/Today I, Carlos, marry you, Anita, my best friend...

Promises about behaviour and relationship: In our marriage I will love, honour, and cherish you/I promise to live with you, to respect you, and honour you/I will be faithful to you/I will stand by your side and sleep in your arms/I will listen to you with compassion and under-standing, and speak to you with encouragement/I prom-ise to respect you, inspire you, and love you...

Changing circumstances: For richer or poorer, in sick-ness and in health/when love is easy and when love is an effort/during good times and bad times, through calm and storms...

Timescale: till death us do part/forever/for the rest of my life/for the whole of our lives together/until love dies/

throughout the adventure of our lives/until the end of time...

Closing intention: This is my solemn promise/and on this promise I base our marriage/this I promise as beats my heart/And it is my intention to keep this promise completely and forever...

From these few lines of example, you can create vows which are traditional or contemporary:

Traditional

In the presence of our family and friends,

*I, Carole, take you, Mario, to be my lawfully
wedded husband.*

I promise to live with you, love you, honour and protect you,

And forsaking all others, be faithful to you

For better for worse,

For richer for poorer,

In sickness and in health

To love and to cherish

Till death us do part.

Contemporary

Today, in this special place,

_I love you with all my heart and I give myself to you
in marriage._

Throughout the ups and downs of life,

I will be patient, honest, and compassionate.

You are my best friend and my equal partner.

I am forever yours, and you are forever mine.

Adding humour

It is okay for your vows to be amusing and light-hearted, particularly if you have a fun and laughter-filled relationship and are playful with each other in how you interact. It might be as simple as including a promise about making her tea in bed every morning, or a promise not to leave your half empty coffee cup laying out in the kitchen. Or you may want to express your vows and promises by writing a quirky poem. Or perhaps you've been inspired by reading the adaptation of the children's book by Dr Seuss, which has been reworked as a set of wedding vows?

It can be tricky to mix very serious romantic language with quirky funny lines, so take the advice of your celebrant if you're trying to do this. And, importantly, make sure that you are not making a joke of, or undermining something that is a legal commitment. So avoid funny comments about only making this commitment under duress – save those for your speeches later on.

Finding the words that are right for YOU

I find that it usually works well to think in detail about your vows from about six months before your wedding. This is a really good time to start collecting meaningful words and phrases – ones that you think describe how you feel about each other, and that sound right for you to say in your vows. Reading wedding poetry or popular prose, and looking at the lyrics of your favourite songs can be a good place to start. You'll soon work out the type of phrases that feel right for you (and the ones that don't!).

However, more than simply looking at phrases and words, try some of these exercises:

Re-writing your memories

Think about the events in your relationship – look back at the stories of the good times and the difficult moments. Write down what happened and what you felt. Was there an evening when you returned home from work tired and grumpy, to find that your partner had cooked your favourite dinner? How did that make you feel? Loved? Cherished, supported, cared for, appreciated? Maybe there was a time when one of you was facing something difficult. Did your partner cheer you up, help you get through it, show understanding and patience, encourage you to speak about it?

You do not need to re-tell the story during your vows or the rest of your ceremony, but when you use the words love, or trust, or honesty, or support in your vows, your brain will link them with the emotions that you felt at the time, and give your declarations and promises real depth of meaning and significance.

Dwelling on what you love about each other

- What is the single greatest thing about the person you are going to marry?

- When did you first feel that you were in love, or know that this person was the one you wanted to spend your life with?

- What will change in your relationship once you are married (if anything)? What will stay the same?

- What is your favourite memory of your partner? It may be a happy moment, something humorous, silly, tender, romantic, heroic, emotional, or simply the look that makes you go weak at the knees.

- What are the most important values or principles on which you would like to base your relationship?

- What promises would you make to each other, if you thought that no-one was listening?

Your life now and in the future

Sometimes, rather than trying to write your actual vows, it can help if you start by jotting down things that you really appreciate about your partner and your life together. For example:

- Write down five things that you'd like to thank him/ her for; anything from making you a cup of tea when you get home from work, to supporting you through a very difficult time.

- Write down five things that you dream of doing with your partner in the future; anything from travelling round the world, to getting a dog.

- Think of the three most important qualities that YOU bring to the relationship, such as honesty, kindness, light-heartedness.

- Think of the best thing that has happened in your relationship when you have had real joy and excitement, and think of the most difficult time when you have supported each other.

- And finally, think about what you want to say about your long-term intention and commitment.

From the answers to some of these questions, you could put together some words to say to each other, that might look like this:

I want to thank you for being in my life, for making my breakfast every morning, and for standing by me when things are tough at work;

I look forward to sharing all my dreams with you, planning our life together, and saving for our fantasy cottage in the country;

I promise always to be kind, to be honest about my feelings, and to be light-hearted when you are down;

I will delight in being with you during good times, when exams are passed and the sun is shining, and I will stick by you when times are tough;

I make this vow to you with the intention of keeping it completely and forever.

Respond, repeat, read or remember?

There are four main options for saying your vows. The first is when everything you want to say is **posed as a question:**

Do you, Donald, accept Catriona as your wife? Do you promise to live with her, love her, comfort and honour her, and be faithful to her, for all time? Donald says: 'I do.'

This is a great option for nervous brides and grooms as it doesn't require you to say too much; you only need to respond to the questions being asked. However, it can be too tempting to make it very simple, where your celebrant or officiant asks one simple question to the groom, and then to the bride – job done! Personally, I think that if there is only one question and one answer, the ceremony may miss out on some of the richness of what the couple feel about each other, and the promises that they want to make to each other on their wedding day. So be inventive in how questions are used...

Alberto and Mira felt very nervous about speaking their vows. Mira had a stammer which was more pronounced if she was stressed, and yet they wanted their vows to be meaningful and heartfelt. They agreed the words that they wanted to say to each other, and then I rephrased them as a question. They answered their legal declaration individually, then made their promises together, making Mira feel more confident about her voice:

Celebrant: Do you, Alberto, take Mira to be your wife: to live together, to love her, comfort and honour her for the rest of your lives together?

Alberto: I do.

Celebrant: Do you, Mira, take Alberto to be your husband: to live together, to love him, comfort and honour him for the rest of your lives together?

Mira: I do.

Alberto and Mira, will you be each other's faithful partner for life?
Will you be each other's constant friend and one true love?

Both answer (together): We will.

Mira and Alberto, do you promise to love each other without reservation?
Will you stand by each other in sickness and health, in plenty and in need?

Both answer (together): We will.

Alberto and Mira, will you share your laughter?
Will you look for the brightness in life and the positive in each other?

Both answer (together): We will.

Mira and Alberto, will you honour each other?

Will you seek to cherish and strengthen your love?

Both answer (together): We will.

Most often, when a couple are saying their vows, I say a line and the couple **repeat it after me**. In some ways this sounds really odd – there is almost no other occasion in our adult life when we do something like this – and yet, is it one of the most effective ways of saying your vows. You only have to recall very short phrases; the timing and the phrasing is slow and smooth because you are following the pace of your celebrant; your guests will be able to hear your celebrant and know what is being said (even if you speak in a very quiet voice to each other); and, best of all, it means that you can look at your partner as you are saying your vows.

If your vows are very personal or very long, it may be simpler for you to **read them to each other**. There is one important maxim here: take it slowly. This is for three reasons – firstly, so that your partner has time to listen and hear and absorb the meaning of what you are saying; secondly, so that your guests have the best chance of hearing what you are saying to each other; and thirdly, to control your own voice and emotions. However calm and in control you think you are when you are practising at home, there is a risk that you might speed up without pause for breath, getting faster and faster the more emotional you feel, and becoming more and more emotional because you are not breathing slowly and deeply. So if you are going to read your vows from a card, here is my advice: practise out loud so that your mouth gets used to saying the words, take it slowly, breathe deeply, and don't make your vows too long...

Maybe you have seen a wonderful romantic film where the couple look into one another's eyes. They say some words which are funny and moving and spontaneous. Oh, don't we wish that could be us! Remember, those lines are being spoken by actors who have learned and rehearsed them, and they've been scripted by an experienced writer.

Spontaneous declarations can be wonderful, but your celebrant or officiant will also want to make sure that you are making a legal declaration, too. If I am working with a couple who want to be spontaneous, then I usually start with the statement that covers the legal requirements, then I can relax and let the couple say what is important.

You may prefer to be like the actor, and **learn and rehearse** your vows so that you are not holding a piece of paper. This looks beautiful on film but can be trickier in reality. Your wedding day is often full of emotion – wonderful emotions, but enough to make it an added burden if you are under pressure to remember important words. I also notice that occasionally when someone is remembering their vows, while they are speaking one line, they are mentally looking around to remember the next line, rather than being able to concentrate fully on the promises that they are making to the person they are marrying.

My advice, if you want to remember your vow, is to practise (often); keep it very short; and make sure your celebrant or officiant has a copy to prompt you if you need it.

Do we have to say the same words?

You might want to say the same vow to each other, or you might want to say something different.

Carl and Shawna chose to write their own vows, but they wanted a similarity in some aspects. They agreed a few phrases which were essential to both of them and used these at the beginning and end of their vows. Then they created the middle section of their vows independently to reflect what each of them considered to be important.

'I love you, Shawna. Today, I give myself to you in marriage. I promise to protect you and inspire you, to laugh with you, and to comfort you in times of sadness. I will listen to you with compassion and understanding, and speak to you with encouragement. I will trust you with my dreams and support you in fulfilling yours. Ahead lies a path filled with adventure and love, and I choose to spend today, and all of my tomorrows, with you. I am forever yours, and you are forever mine.'

'I love you, Carl. Today, I give myself to you in marriage, to live with you, and laugh with you. To stand by your side, and sleep in your arms. I will trust you with my dreams and support you as you strive to achieve your goals. I vow to love you in good times and in bad, when life seems easy and when it seems hard. I promise to be patient, honest, and compassionate with you; to be your best friend and your sweetheart. I will love you with all my heart for my whole life. I choose to spend today, and all of my tomorrows, with you. I am forever yours and you are forever mine.'

Using Poetry

Sometimes we find a piece of prose or a poem which is beautifully written, and sums up so exactly what we feel that we want to include it in our ceremony. It can be very effective to use a piece like this as your vow. It may be a piece of poetry which is relatively unknown and personal to you, or it may be something more popular. Chris and Karen made a beautiful adaptation of Rudyard Kipling's poem, 'If'. They said alternate verses to each other as their vow, and then concluded with: 'If we can keep two passions burning bright and work together to achieve our goals, then I will marry you, and I will marry you, and we will have a strong and lasting marriage.'

Some examples to inspire you

Hopefully, you have been inspired by all those choices rather than scared. Your vows do not have to be poetic to be effective. The most important thing is that they state your true feelings of love and commitment with sincerity, and reflect your own personality.

I've added some examples that cover the traditional, the contemporary, the romantic and the practical. As with other sections of this book, I suggest you highlight the words or phrases you love, and ignore or cross out those that you think sound too formal or too cheesy! Mix and match words, phrases, and structures and let yourself be creative.

(And of course, wherever it says 'Bride' or 'Groom', replace it with your names.)

Traditional Vows

Celebrant: Groom, do you take Bride to be your wife, to live together, to love her, comfort and honour her; and, forsaking all others, keep only to her, so long as you both shall live?

Groom: I do.

Celebrant: Bride, do you take Groom to be your husband, to live together, to love him, comfort and honour him; and, forsaking all other, keep only to him, so long as you both shall live?

Bride: I do

Bride and Groom hold hands at look at each other and repeat after the Celebrant:

I, Groom, take you, Bride, to be my wife,

to have and to hold from this day forward,

for better for worse,

for richer for poorer,

in sickness and in health,

to love and to cherish, till death us do part.

(and this I promise as beats my heart).

I, Bride, take you, Groom, to be my husband,

to have and to hold from this day forward,

for better for worse,

for richer for poorer,

in sickness and in health,

to love and to cherish, till death us do part,

(and this is my solemn vow).

(OR, and upon this promise I will base our marriage; OR, to love and to cherish forever; OR, to love and to cherish for all of my life.)

Statement followed by promise

I want to say thank you, in front of all my family and friends, for being in my life, for loving me, and for wanting to share your life with me. It sometimes seems like a miracle, because I didn't know I could be so happy. You have given me more than I could ever imagine, and I promise that I will always try to support you, understand you, trust you, and work with you to build our marriage and our future together.

Simple appreciations followed by promise

I (name) accept you (name) as my husband/wife/partner because...

(listing the reasons and qualities you love and admire)

and I promise to...

(love, be faithful, care for, understand...)

through...

(good and bad times, sunshine and shadows, sickness and health, abundance and scarcity...)

Contemporary Vows

In the presence of our family and friends,

I (name) choose you (name) to be my wife/husband/spouse/partner.

From this day forward, I vow

To love and care for you

To be a comfort to you

To listen to you

To learn and grow with you.

I give you my love,

I give you my heart,

I give you my hope,

I give you my joy,

For the rest of the days of my life.

OR

I, (name), take you, (name), to be my husband/wife,

To share all that I am and all that I have,

For all time to come.

And to keep our love as deep and as strong as it is today.

As your husband/wife,

I promise to care for you,

trust your love,

be responsive to your needs,

communicate my feelings,

and behave in a way that shows my love and respect.

I make this promise because I love you,

and want to live out the days of my life with you.

OR

In front of these witnesses, I make my promise to you

To love you freely

To love you purely

To love you joyfully

To love you truly

I will love you always

From this day forward and forever.

OR

With our family and friends as witnesses,

I make my solemn promise

To love you and hold you as my wife (husband/partner)

To stand beside you in good times and bad.

OR

With our family and friends as our witness,

I (name) take you (name), from this day forward and into the future

To be my partner, my friend, my husband/wife.

To walk by your side

Through sickness and health,

Through prosperity and uncertainty,

When love is easy and when love is an effort,

I commit to our life together as a team.

I choose you and I love you.

I promise always to hold you in the highest regard, to respect you, and to be your faithful husband (wife/partner).

OR

I, (name), take you, (name), to be my wife/husband.

To love you when you drive me crazy,

To respect you when we disagree,

To support you if bad times come our way,

And to always remember how grateful I am

To have you by my side.

OR

(Name), I promise to walk by your side and support and encourage you.

I promise to love and accept all parts of you.

I celebrate us and what we have together today,

And vow to continue celebrating our love throughout the years ahead.

OR

Today I honour and thank you for all that you are to me,

All that you've given me and all that we share together.

Thank you for your openness and honesty.

I will love you and respect you all our days together.

OR

(name), I take you to be my husband/wife,

To share our laughter,

To kiss away the tears,

And to give you all the love in my heart,

As long as we both shall live.

OR

From this day onward, I choose you (name) to be my husband/wife,

To live together and laugh together,

To work by your side and dream in your arms,

To fill your heart and feed your soul,

To always seek out the best in you,

And to love you with all my heart.

OR

I, (name) take you (name) to be my husband/wife.

You are my companion in life and my one true love.

I will treasure our friendship and love you today, tomorrow, and forever.

I will trust and honour you, I will laugh and cry with you,

I will love you faithfully through the best and the worst, through the difficult and the easy.

What may come, I will always be there.

As I have given you my hands to hold,

So I give you my life to cherish.

OR

As we go through life together,

I will be your lover, companion, and friend,

your greatest fan and your toughest adversary,

your comrade in adventure,

your student and your teacher,

your consolation in disappointment,

your accomplice in mischief,

your strength in times of need,

and, most of all, your love throughout all time.

OR

Thank you for wanting to be my wife/husband/partner.

Before our friends and family here with us today,

I declare to you my firm and clear intentions.

I will sustain for all our lives my love and care for you, and offer you support in every way I can.

I will strive to give you what you want and need from me, and help you become the person you wish to be.

I will work with you to build and maintain a loving and healthy home for ourselves and our children.

OR

I promise to give you the best of myself, and to ask of you no more than you can give.

I promise to respect you as your own person, and to realise that your interests, desires, and needs are no less important than my own.

I promise to share with you my time and my attention, and to bring joy, strength, and imagination to our relationship.

I promise to keep myself open to you, to let you see through the window of my world into my innermost fears and feelings, secrets and dreams.

I promise to grow along with you, to be willing to face changes in order to keep our relationship alive and exciting.

I promise to love you in good times and bad, with all I have to give and all I feel inside in the only way I know how, completely and forever.

What do YOU want?

- Important words for inclusion in the vows:

- Favourite lines, phrases, styles:

Chapter 5: Rings and Other Tokens

With this ring I thee wed...

For hundreds – and maybe thousands – of years, couples have been using rings during a wedding ceremony as a public pledge and to honour a marriage. Since Egyptian times, a circle has been seen as a symbol of eternity – with no beginning and no end – and the hole in the centre of a ring was symbolic of a gateway, leading to the future and to events known or unknown.

Later, in Chapter 8, you can read about other symbolic gestures and rituals, but in the 21st Century exchanging rings is one of the most frequently used gestures and I think it merits a chapter of its own.

Customs and History

A wedding ring is seen as one of the most universal symbols in the world, and it carries the same symbolic significances almost everywhere. But what it is made of, and how it is worn varies across countries and cultures.

In Western cultures, a wedding ring is most frequently worn on the fourth finger of the left hand, giving its name to the 'ring finger'. At different periods in history, rings have been worn on the right hand and worn on the thumb or other fingers. Some Jewish traditions involve the groom placing a ring on the bride's index finger, and in some countries – including Russia, Greece, Poland, Austria, Portugal, and Norway – it was customary to wear a wedding ring on the right hand.

There is a story from ancient times that there is a vein which runs directly from the ring finger to the heart, and the Romans even named it *Vena Amoris* or vein of love, to show the connection between a wedding ring and true love! In fact, it may simply be more practical, to avoid damage to the ring and to prevent it from getting in the way of work, to wear a ring on the finger which is the least used, and on the non-dominant hand. Some people who are left-handed choose to wear their wedding ring on the opposite hand.

Often rings are relatively plain bands of gold, platinum, or other precious metal, but I've held weddings where the rings were made of wood, leather, or other materials; often something which is meaningful to the couple. In Roman times, wedding rings were often decorated with a key to symbolise the unlocking of the heart, and the Victorians decorated rings with gemstones: Diamond, Emerald, Amethyst, Ruby, Emerald, Sapphire and Turquoise, spelling out 'DEAREST'.

Diamonds have been used in wedding rings throughout history. The word originates from the Greek word *Adamas*, which means unconquerable and signifies enduring love, and many gems carry a symbolic significance which you might like to factor into your choice:

Diamond:	strong, enduring relationships and balanced-thinking
Sapphire:	commitment, loyalty, honesty and truth
Ruby:	peace, power and love
Emerald:	rebirth, fertility, love and eternal youth
Opal:	inspiration, hope and purity
Pearl:	the moon, feminine beauty, ultimate perfection
Amethyst:	calmness and emotional wellbeing
Topaz:	protection and personal strength
Aquamarine:	friendship and faithfulness

One ring or two?

During much of the 19th and 20th centuries, it was customary for only the bride to wear a wedding ring. This started to change during the Second World War, when many couples were separated soon after their marriage and dual rings became more popular, so that, even if they were far away, the couple could carry their love with them.

In the 1960s and 1970s, it became more acceptable for men to wear jewellery, and the popularity of both men and women wearing rings increased. Now it is very usual for both parties to wear a ring, and the marriage is seen as a celebration of equal commitment.

But, whichever hand the ring(s) will be worn on, and whatever it is made of, there are several things to think about when incorporating rings into a wedding ceremony.

Bringing the rings into the ceremony

It is traditional that one of the duties of the best man is to look after the rings before the wedding, and to hand them to the officiant during the ceremony. Sometimes the couple don't trust the best man not to lose them, and something there are other choices about bringing the rings to the ceremony. Often a small child, maybe a page boy, will be a ring-bearer, arriving with the bride and her attendants with the rings on a cushion (securely tied!) and handing them to the best man or officiant once they reach the top of the aisle.

Sarah and Ewan had a lovely old Labrador, Monty, who was an important part of their day-to-day lives. They wanted Monty to be with them on their wedding day so he didn't have to go into kennels, and they had chosen a lovely outdoor venue which was happy for dogs to be included.

During the ceremony, Monty was being looked after by a guest sitting in the back row, and most of the time Monty lay under a chair in the shade. When it came time for Ewan and Sarah to exchange rings, Monty was encouraged from his place and he plodded down the aisle, delivering the rings on a tartan cushion which was attached to his collar. It was a lovely moment, and it meant a lot to Sarah and Ewan to include their faithful pet in their wedding.

Ewan and Sarah were fortunate in that Monty had a calm nature and was used to being in crowded events. However, I do urge caution about having dogs, or other animals, involved in your ceremony. Even calm pets get a sense of the excitement that is going on, and they can either become scared and hide nervously under a chair, or they become over-excited, rushing around and jumping up – and most brides do not want muddy paws on their dress before the ceremony starts. During one wedding, the couple's dog clearly wanted to be with the bride, and the bride's mother spent most of the ceremony paying attention to the animal, trying to get it to sit quietly, not bark, and to stop it from pulling on its lead, straining to reach its owners. I really think the bride's mum would have rather sat peacefully and watched her daughter get married.

Another increasingly popular way to deliver the rings is to have an owl fly in with them (the rings are usually in a little pouch attached to its leg). The best man stands with a gauntlet on his hand, and the owl swoops silently in and lands on his gloved arm so the rings can be retrieved, before flying back to its handler at the back of the room. Of course, with any living creature, things can go wrong, and I've seen an owl fly up into the rafters rather than to the best man. There are also many people with a phobia of birds, and you may unnerve some of your guests by having a flying bird in a small space. So even if you are an ardent fan of Harry Potter, think carefully before using animals, and always use a reputable bird handler and trainer.

Ring Cushions

Often the rings are in a simple box or bag, but sometimes a couple have chosen to have a ring cushion to display the rings, or to have them presented in another way, such as in a copy of a book with a section cut out of the pages so that the rings are kept securely in place. When I married Amanda and Jim, they had been having a discussion about a potential ring-bearer. Jim had mis-heard and he was struggling to understand the concept of a 'ring-bear', so as a surprise Amanda had bought a stuffed teddy bear, tied the rings around its neck, and during the ceremony the page boy presented the ring-bear to Jim. ☺

A ring cushion or other carrier can be an opportunity to personalise your wedding in a subtle way. I've seen cushions made with the handkerchief of a much-loved grandmother who couldn't attend the wedding, and I've had rings presented in music boxes, a bird's nest, a family heirloom snuff box, and tied to a carved wooden stick.

However the rings are presented, make sure that the best man can easily retrieve them or untie them – you don't want the rings falling loose or getting lost, but neither do you want them tied on with tight, fiddly knots, requiring a pair of scissors to be found in the middle of the ceremony.

Blessing the rings

Often the celebrant or officiant will say a few words before rings are exchanged. This might be about the symbolism of the rings, the fact of them being a visible sign of the promises the couple have made, or maybe the shared values that they represent, such as commitment, love, honesty or trust.

A lovely way to include your family and friends in your ceremony is to have a ring warming or ring blessing. During the ceremony, or before it starts, the rings which you will exchange are passed amongst all your guests. As they hold them in their hands, they pause for a moment, silently making their blessings or good wishes for the couple, and then pass them on to the next person. This can be done with all your guests participating, or if there are too many people, or you think that some joker might find it funny to swap the ring for an alternative, then the rings might be passed amongst closest family members or only the bridal party. I usually start this process early on in the ceremony so there is time for the rings to be passed around everyone while the rest of the ceremony is taking place, starting with the bride's family and being returned eventually to the best man. Then, when you exchange rings, you know that they carry with them the blessings and good wishes of your family and friends, and their love, hope, and support for your marriage.

What to say

The most traditional of wedding ceremonies uses the words:

With this ring I thee wed,

With my body I thee honour,

And with all my worldly goods I thee endow.

And the most frequently used words are:

I give you this ring as a symbol of our marriage.

All that I am, I give to you.

All that I have, I share with you

For the whole of our life together.

Both of these signify the giving of everything of one's self and also everything that you possess, and here is a version which conveys the same sentiments but in more contemporary language:

With this ring, I marry you.

All that I have, all that I am,

All of my past, present and future, are yours and mine,

And I love you.

Most frequently, your celebrant will lead you, and you will be asked to repeat the words line by line after them. Or if the words you choose are very short, you may want to memorise them. If you don't want to say much, ask your celebrant to make your chosen lines into a question for you to answer 'yes', 'I will' or 'I do' (or anything else that's meaningful for you), or simply ask the celebrant to direct you to exchange rings as a sign of your love and a visible reminder of the promises you have made.

Some people choose to say something only when they give the ring, others choose also to say something as they accept the ring. This symbolises that love cannot just be given, but has to be willingly received as well.

(as you place the ring on your partner's finger): This ring is a token of my love. I marry you and give you all that I have and all that I am.

Response (once the ring is on your finger): I will forever wear this ring as a sign of my commitment.

OR

I give you this ring as a symbol of my love. As it encircles your finger, may it remind you always that you are surrounded by my love.

Response: I will wear it gladly. Whenever I look at it, I will remember this day and the vows we have made.

Some examples to inspire you

I've added here some examples that cover the traditional, the contemporary, the romantic, and the practical. As with other sections of this book, highlight the words or phrases you love, and ignore or cross out those that you think sound too formal or too cheesy! Mix and match words, phrases and structures, and let yourself be creative.

I give you this ring as a symbol of my love and faithfulness. As I place it on your finger, I commit my heart to you. Wear this ring as a reminder of the vows we have made today.

OR

I give you this ring to wear with love and joy. As a ring has no end, neither shall my love for you. I choose you to be my (wife/husband/partner) this day and forever.

OR

I give you this ring that you may wear it as a reminder of my love for you.

OR

I give you this ring as a reminder that I will love, honour, and cherish you – in all times, in all places, and in all ways, forever.

OR

*I give you this ring as a symbol of my love and
devotion. I offer you my heart, my hand, and my love.*

OR

*With this ring, I pledge my love and faithfulness to
you, today, tomorrow, and always.*

OR

*With this ring, I marry you and join my life with
yours. Accept this ring as a sign of my love and
faithfulness for all the years to come.*

OR

*This ring I give to you as a token of my love and
devotion to you. I pledge to you all that I am and all
that I will ever be as your (husband/wife). With this
ring, I gladly marry you and join my life to yours.*

OR

*This ring of precious metal symbolises that your love
is the most precious element in my life. The ring is
a circle with no beginning and no end, to show that
the love between us will never cease. I place it on
your finger as a sign of the vows which have made us
husband and wife.*

OR

*I give this ring as my gift to you, a symbol of all that
we have promised and all that we shall share. Wear it
and think of me, and know that I love you.*

OR

I give you this ring as a visible and constant symbol of my promise to be with you as long as I live.

OR

I give you this ring as a symbol of my love for you. Let it be a reminder that I am always by your side, and that I will always be a faithful partner to you.

OR

Let this ring be a symbol of my promises to you and a reminder of my devotion to you. I am honoured to call you my (wife/husband/partner).

OR

I give you this ring to wear as a symbol of my abiding love, my eternal faith, and my undying devotion. It is an outward reminder of our inner unity.

OR

This ring I give you is a symbol of my love. I pledge to share with you my heart, my home, and everything I own.

Practicalities

Putting a ring onto someone else's finger can feel very unnatural – the ring is probably a snug fit, and it is difficult to know how much pressure to exert without hurting the person you are marrying. Add to that warm hands, perhaps a little sweaty due to nervousness, and even the best fitting ring can be difficult to put on. If it feels tricky, twist the ring a little as you push it, and if all else fails leave it placed above the knuckle and the wearer can push it on further themselves.

It always helps if you assist your partner by holding out the correct hand and the correct finger for the ring to go on. I've seen brides with the nail on their ring finger decorated with sparkly polish to differentiate it from the rest. I've also officiated at a wedding where the groom, Wilson, stuck out his right hand rather than his left, and only realised his mistake when he was signing the marriage paperwork and he couldn't get the ring off to put it on his left hand!

What to do with your engagement ring?

Because engagement rings are often more ornate than wedding rings, they are usually placed on the finger after the wedding ring. Most often the bride will come to the wedding with her engagement ring either on her other hand, or will have given it to someone else for safe-keeping.

Selina and Gordon had a lovely engagement story. Selina's mother had given Gordon the diamonds from her grandmother's ring and Gordon had got them made into a new ring for Selena. For the proposal, he took her on a surprise trip to the country where her grandmother had been born, and they became engaged at the family farm. Selina and Gordon didn't want the engagement ring to be slipped back on quietly, and wanted to incorporate it into their ceremony. This is what we said: 'The ring with which Gordon and Selina were engaged, has special significance to them. An engagement ring is a symbol of promise and intention. Today that intention is realised and the promise has been fulfilled. So, Gordon, this is your opportunity to re-place the engagement ring on Selina's finger, this time above her wedding band, to symbolise that the love that brought you together will always protect and sustain your marriage." (Then Gordon put the engagement ring on Selina's finger.)

Blessing of the Hands

During the exchange of rings, everyone's attention is on the couple's hands, and immediately after the rings have been put on can be a lovely time to include a blessing. This acknowledges that hands which during the wedding are adorned with a ring, are also the hands which through-out the couple's life will be part of the routine of care, comfort, and loving touch.

You can choose phrases which suit you and your life-style best, or you may like to include one of the following examples:

(names of couple), look at the hands that are holding yours today: These are the hands that will love and cherish you through the years; these are the hands that will work alongside yours, as together you build your future; these are the hands that will give you strength if you struggle through difficult times; these are the hands that will support you and encourage you to follow your dreams; these are the hands that you hold today in joy, and excitement, and hope.

OR

Your hands are joined, and with them your hearts. These are the hands of the one you love and adore. On this day, you have promised to love and honour one another for all your days.

Reaching out to the one you love, may you find strength. Standing side by side, may you find partnership. Sharing responsibilities and chores, may you find equality and support. Helping each other in daily life and work, may you find fulfilment. Loving each other through good and bad times, may you find endurance. As you hold hands together, our wish for you is that you build an extraordinary life together.

OR

May your hands be always clasped in friendship. May they have the strength to hold on during times of stress. May they be tender and gentle as they nurture your love. May they continue to build a relationship rich in caring. May your hands together work as healer, protector, shelter, and guide.

OR

The hands you hold today are the hands of your best friend; young and strong and full of love for you, as you promise to love each other today, tomorrow, and forever. They will comfort you if you are sad. As years pass, they will tenderly hold your children and keep the whole of your family together. And when you are older, wrinkled and aged, these hands will still be reaching for yours, still giving you the same unspoken tenderness with just a touch.

Alternatives to Wedding Rings

Of course not everyone wants to exchange rings. The symbolism of rings may be at odds with your values and beliefs, you may work in a job where it is not practical or possible to wear a ring, or you may simply not like to wear jewellery.

Some people will accept them as part of the ceremony but then rarely wear them again. This can be the case with people who don't much like jewellery, or who do a lot of sport or outdoor activities. Temporary rings might work for some couples. For example, a ring woven from flax or other plant material could be used during the wedding as a token gesture that does not need to be worn after the wedding, or rings made from lace or tartan. This might be nice if the material you use has a cultural or personal meaning, if you're both nature lovers, or if you simply love plants.

I have held weddings where couples have chosen to exchange other symbolic gifts, for example, necklaces, or a charm bracelet which can be added to throughout life.

Gemma and Paul were busy doctors. They were both training to become specialised in their respective fields, and their life was full of difficult shift hours and studying for exams. Part of the commitment they made to each other in their vows was to ensure that each of them deliberately made time to spend with the other person – trying to arrange similar shift patterns when they could and putting aside their books sometimes, so they could enjoy each other's company. They decided not to exchange rings but they wanted to symbolise the gift of time, so during their ceremony they gave each other a watch.

Recently, I have held some weddings where the couples celebrated their marriage with a tattoo – one couple had wedding rings tattooed on their fingers, and another had the date of their wedding in roman numerals on their arms.

Other alternatives include planting a tree, having your names and wedding date carved in rock, or giving something else which includes a diamond. Jaya gave Phil a diamond-tipped drill bit, which was much more useful for him than a ring; and when Pete and Enya were married, they commissioned an ornament with two crystal swans – birds which are reputed to mate for life.

When Zoe and Frank were married, they decided that they didn't want any physical representation of their marriage. Instead, after they had said their vows, the guests gathered around them – the physical circle representing the love of family and friends which encircled the couple.

A final word on rings...

Although rings are symbolic gifts, and precious mementoes, they are small and removable, and therefore liable to get lost. My husband and I have both lost our wedding rings – mine is somewhere in our garden, and my husband lost his while we were white water rafting in Costa Rica. On each occasion we felt extremely sad and a bit unsettled by the loss of a physical emblem and a unique treasure from our wedding day. We were uncertain what to do about replacing them... until we discovered a workshop where we could make our own rings. So over the course of a few weeks, we chose a piece of gold and I made a new ring for him and he made a new ring for me. Of course they cannot replace completely the rings we exchanged at our wedding, but they represent an ongoing commitment, and we have a new story to tell.

What do YOU want?

- Will you exchange rings? Something else of significance?

- Who will be responsible for bringing them?

- Important words for inclusion in the exchange:

- Favourite lines, phrases, styles:

Chapter 6: Choosing Music

All you need is Love...

There is something magical about the moment when I ask guests to be ready for the arrival of the bridal party. The conversations cease, there is hushed anticipation, and then the music starts – those first few notes can be quite spine-tingling in how they set the mood. Whether it is an organ blasting out the first few bars of the traditional wedding march, the smooth sound of a cello or harp playing something classical and romantic, or the upbeat sound of something more contemporary, music is one of the best expressions of human emotion.

You may already have given time and thought to the playlist for your evening reception, but may not have considered how to add personality and atmosphere during the ceremony. Personalising your selection of music can add greatly to the wedding, and to the mood of the ceremony as it progresses.

This chapter does not suggest a definitive list of all the possible music choices – that is a task for you to enjoy with your partner – but, instead, I hope to guide you through the kind of decisions you will need to make and the issues you should consider.

Choosing your selections

If you're having a religious ceremony, you may be restricted in what you can play. If your ceremony is not religious, your music options are more open to classical and contemporary tunes. Either way, be sure to discuss your music selections with your celebrant or officiant so they know what to expect, how to introduce the music, and how to co-ordinate with the musicians on the day.

In general, a wedding ceremony has five main places where music might be played:

Before the ceremony: During the 15-30 minutes before the ceremony, as your guests are arriving. This music welcomes the guests, and is the background by which they're seated and while they are waiting for the wedding to begin. Some couples choose background music to avoid the guests sitting in a silent room, but if your wedding has a particular mood or theme then the choice of appropriate music can help to build the mood and create anticipation even before the wedding starts.

Roseanne and Sean were planning a wedding with a strong Scottish theme. There was a piper playing bagpipes outside to welcome the guests, and inside there were Scottish folk tunes being played on the fiddle and accordion as guests took their seats. Even before the ceremony started, feet were tapping and guests were ready to sing along and to dance.

Arrival of the bridal party: This music sets the pace for the attendants and the bride, or the couple, walking down the aisle – this is the moment all the guests have been waiting for. Choose a song that makes you and your partner happy and celebratory, or which feels romantic and beautiful – whether that means traditional time-honoured classics, such as Wagner's *Bridal Chorus* (*Here Comes the Bride*), rocking down the aisle to *You're My Best Friend* by Queen, or enjoying a sedate walk to the romantic sound of Pachelbel's *Canon in D*.

Some couples plan a change of music for each portion of the procession; one piece for the bridesmaids, then another for the entrance of the bride. However, in many venues the aisle is too short for this to be effective. It takes a surprisingly short time to walk the length of a room, and changing music means that the bride may arrive at the front while the music is still in its opening bars. Standing waiting while the music continues for a full minute or more feels like an incredibly long time for a nervous bride and groom.

If your music has a particular high point, make sure you time your entrance to match your favourite section. For example, *One Day Like This,* by Elbow, doesn't reach a crescendo until almost two minutes into the track. On the other hand, you don't want your music to end too soon, leaving you walking in silence!

During the ceremony: As part of your ceremony, there might be communal singing of a hymn or other song; or a choir or soloist may sing as an identified part of the ceremony; or there may be music accompanying another element of the ceremony, for example, during the lighting of a unity candle or while the legal paperwork is being signed.

This can be a great opportunity for someone to be involved – during Kim and Dominic's wedding, Kim's brother played the ukulele and sang *Somewhere Over the Rainbow* while the couple were completing their legal paperwork. It was a wonderful rendition and it helped maintain the continuity of the ceremony, so even though the couple were busy attending to the formalities, the ceremony continued without a break. By way of contrast, Bob and Matilda chose more contemporary music, with *Signed, Sealed, Delivered* by Stevie Wonder.

Recessional: This is the music at the end of the ceremony; the triumphant moment when the bride and groom leave as a newly-married couple. It is usually upbeat and joyous, and is louder and quicker than other pieces of music in the ceremony. Classical choices include Beethoven's *Ode to Joy*, Vivaldi's *Four Seasons*, and Handel's *Water Music*. You will want to create a real celebratory feel, so have the volume loud enough so that it can be heard over the clapping and cheering of your guests, and maybe even choose a piece of music that makes you feel like dancing down the aisle – *Another One Bites the Dust*, or *All You Need is Love*, or the music from *Star Wars…*

As the guests leave: A continuation of upbeat and celebratory music will keep your guests feeling they're a part of the wedding until they have all filed out of the ceremony space. Beyond this, you may choose to have music continuing on during a drinks reception.

Live music or recorded music?

Without a doubt, live music during your ceremony can add to mood, but also to the cost – unless you are fortunate enough to have talented friends or family who can perform. Whether you choose a string quartet, a singer, a harpist or a bagpiper, having live music gives you more flexibility on the timing of pieces at key stages. If the aisle is short, the musicians can fade out their playing as the bride arrives at the front. Or if the signing of the legal documents and the associated photography takes longer than expected, the musicians can extend their playing or even play another piece.

If you are using musicians, work with them on your music choices. They will have a wealth of experience and can often tell you the kind of pieces that work well – their repertoire may even include beautiful tunes that you are not familiar with. Often, they will have samples of music that you can listen to that will help you make your choices. If you want them to play anything unusual, give them plenty of notice so they can source the music and have time to practise.

Usually, on the day of your wedding, before the ceremony starts your celebrant and your musicians will co-ordinate their plans so that the music is perfectly timed with the rest of your ceremony.

Perhaps you have friends or relatives who are vocalists or who play instruments. Asking them to play or sing is a great way to include people in your ceremony and to add a very personal touch to the proceedings. When Commi and Bruce got married, Bruce had arranged a surprise ending for the ceremony. Commi's family included lots of talented musicians, and her brother played with a band. Commi and Bruce had discussed having the band play during their evening reception, but they had agreed that it would be too much pressure for Commi's brother and that he should be able to enjoy the event as a guest. However, as Bruce and

> *Commi stood facing their guests, and I presented them as husband and wife, the door opened and Commi's brother and the band burst into the room and played a couple of brilliant tracks. Commi was delighted and the whole room were on their feet, clapping along and dancing. It was a stunning conclusion to the ceremony.*

Who is in charge of playing recorded music?

The advantage of having opted for recorded music is that, of course, you have a much greater choice. There is an endless range of styles and pieces, and you can vary your music throughout the ceremony, including the sound of a full orchestra for the bride's arrival, a choir singing during the ceremony, and a famous guitar solo playing at the end. All of it is possible at the touch of a few buttons.

One of the key questions for you to consider is who is going to be in charge of pressing those buttons – will it be someone at the venue, or will it be a task that has been allocated to a guest? However tempted you are, please don't try to take on this task yourself. In planning a wedding, the music is often a task that the groom is happy to take responsibility for. Imagine the situation where the groom has the ceremony music downloaded onto his phone. In the short time before the ceremony, his attention is suddenly required in three places at once: the photographer looking for some shots of the groom and his groomsmen; the celebrant checking final paperwork or that the key guests are in place; and the person who is organising the music trying to get to grips with an unfamiliar phone and find the correct tracks. Too often this is a task left until the last minute. It is much better to allow plenty of time for the person who is in charge of the music to know how to switch your device on and off, how to find the correct track, how to control the volume, and how to fade the music in and out.

I'll add a further note of caution about using music downloaded onto a phone...

> Boxed text: When Pep and Carla were getting married, Pep had done a wonderful job of selecting music, every piece had been chosen thoughtfully, and the choreography had been timed to perfection. Pep thought he'd barred incoming calls but he'd either forgotten to do it, or the technology had failed him. So in the midst of the candle lighting ritual, the music of Ave Maria was interrupted by the ringing of Pep's phone – amplified through the sound system. There were a lot of flustered attempts to reject the call, and the beautiful music continued. Unfortunately, the caller had left a voicemail message, so of course the phone rang again, and then again...

It is a much safer idea to have songs downloaded and your phone on flight-mode setting, or to have a CD or MP3 with a clear list and the music tracks in order; this planning is incredibly helpful for whoever is in charge of the music.

Sometimes couples ask for a rehearsal of the ceremony, as they are anxious about where people will stand or want to check the order of the events. However, of all the things that need to be practised, my strong suggestion is that the person who is working the music has a run-through. Don't overestimate how tech savvy your friends are when it comes to playing music at an event like this. A rehearsal helps to avoid a long silence waiting for the music to start, or to find that the volume is so quiet that it can barely be heard in a room full of people. It is surprising how much sound is muffled once 70 guests are in the room.

If a staff member at the venue is co-ordinating the music, make sure they have the music early, and try to ensure that the person doing this task is someone experienced. I've worked at some really great venues where everyone is professional and attentive, and I've also held ceremonies where the seemingly 'easy' job of switching the music on and off is given to an inexperienced staff member who cuts the music off suddenly instead of fading the volume out, or who is not paying attention at key points resulting in a delay in the music starting or having the music play on long after the bride has arrived at the front of the aisle.

What kind of music suits your venue?

The setting of your ceremony may have an impact on the type of music you choose. For example: a historic castle might be well matched with the haunting sound of some-one playing the bagpipes; a harp or flute might work well in an elegant hotel; and a for a relaxed outdoor wedding, two friends playing guitars and singing might be the most appropriate choice.

You will also want to pay attention to the acoustics. I've attended weddings where the sound of a single violin was blown away during a windy wedding on a beach, or where the sound of bagpipes reverberating in a low ceilinged room had guests covering their ears, and some children almost in tears – it didn't help that on that occa-sion, the piper was not very good! If you have a sound system, make time for a sound check and have someone in charge of the volume. You might have planned lovely music, but it can fall a bit flat if no-one can hear it properly, or if it is so loud that it drowns out everything else.

Make sure you discuss with the venue and your celebrant where the musicians will be placed during the ceremony. They will need sufficient space for their instrument and music stands, and they will want to be within sight of the celebrant so that they can see the cues for music starting or stopping.

Don and Cissy were married in a wonderful historic chapel. The room was small, and the venue manager advised that the maximum number of guests was 50. Cissy and Don adhered to this, but they hadn't factored in the addition of a harpist (with a full size harp), two photographers, a videographer, and a significant train on the bridal gown. In order to avoid us all tripping over each other, or the photographs being obscured by the bridal party in the small space, we had a last minute change to the seating plan. To fit everyone in comfortably, we had to remove more than half the seats, so some guests were seated near the front and the rest were standing towards the back of the room. Fortunately, the arrangement suited the relaxed and informal style of Don and Cissy's wedding, but it did require some quick thinking in the last few minutes before the bride arrived – and some swift furniture removal by the staff at the castle.

Matching the music to the style of your wedding

Perhaps you have a favourite song, or you are having a very traditional wedding so traditional song choices will be the best match. Maybe you know what music was played at your parents' wedding, or your grandparents', and you want to replicate that.

Music for small weddings can be particularly important – the arrival into the room is likely to be quicker. Even if you're planning the tiniest of weddings – just the bridal party and the celebrant – music can enhance and play an important part. When Susannah and Wilson were married, they had music playing throughout the ceremony. They chose a long instrumental piece which ran continuously for 30 minutes. It started quietly for a couple of minutes before the ceremony, increased in volume as the bride and groom arrived together, played very quietly in the background for the duration of the ceremony and then increased in volume again as the marriage was pronounced and the couple kissed. It was one of the most romantic weddings I've held, and with the musical accompaniment it felt like we were in a film-set.

Communal singing

If you are being married in a church, you will most likely want to include hymns. But if you are having a wedding which is not religious, or you are getting married in another venue, you will have to decide whether you want guests to be involved and to join in with singing.

I find that this can be one of the most awkward elements of a wedding. If guests are attending a wedding in a church, they will arrive with an expectation that some hymn singing might be included. However, if you have chosen another venue, that expectation is not so strong, and particularly if it is a small wedding. Remember that people who are normally strong singers may find that the emotion of the day has an impact on their ability to sing, or they might feel uncomfortable singing in a small group.

Often hymn singing is best accompanied by the musicians at your wedding, or you may want to consider having a professional to lead the singing. As an alternative, some couples choose to play a recorded version, with guests singing along and joining in. However your song or hymn is accompanied, be careful about the pitch and speed; some hymns and popular songs cover a difficult range from low to high.

Monica and Matt wanted to include the same hymn as had been sung at Monica's parents' wedding. They did not have musicians, so they chose a recording of the hymn with the intention that guests would sing along. The version they chose was sung by a Welsh male voice choir. As a piece of music it was stunning; but, as something for people to join in with, it was impossible. The speed of the hymn was very slow and grand, as befits that type of choir, and each note at the end of a line was held for an inordinate length of time. By the time we'd got through the first verse and chorus, it was clear that people couldn't sing along. In fact, guests were starting to giggle with the effort of trying to take a big enough breath to follow the phrasing and hold onto the notes. So we all sat down, and for the rest of the hymn we listened and could enjoy the wonderful singing of the choir without trying to match it.

Unless your celebrant or officiant is a confident leader of singing, it is always a wise idea to have someone nominated to lead the singing. This may be a professional singer, but if it is one or more of your guests, have them come to the front to provide a clear lead, and choose someone who is confident about hitting the high notes, enthusiastic, and a bit of an extrovert – not a reluctant volunteer, or someone who is likely to feel shy or emotional.

As an alternative to hymns, there are some lovely songs which work well for community singing and add to the joyful atmosphere. *Walking on Sunshine* by Katrina and the Waves, *Your Love Keeps Lifting Me Higher* (Jackie Wilson), *Stand by Me* (Ben E King), and the Beatles classic, *All You Need is Love*, have all worked well at recent weddings I've attended. And at one wedding there was a selection of children's shakers, tambourines and kazoos, so that even those who were not good singers could join in and contribute to the noise.

Make sure you have copies of the words for the bridal party, including the bride and groom – trying to sing along when you don't have the words, or the correct version, is a bit difficult. And remember copyright rules. Some commercial printers will not include words of a song if you do not have copyright permission to re-print them in your order of service.

What do YOU want?

- Favourite songs

- Favourite music artists

- What type of music suits the venue and the style of our wedding?

- Options for arrival music

Jane Patmore

- Options for recessional

- Other music (hymns, song recital or instrumental, communal singing, music during the signing of the legal paperwork)

- Who will be in charge of music co-ordination on the day?

Chapter 7: Choosing Readings

'Poetry is when an emotion has found its thought and the thought has found words.' **Robert Frost**

There are many beautiful words in books and songs and poems, and having a guest to read at your wedding is a lovely way to pick up on the meaning of love and marriage, and the way you feel about each other. Finding the right poems, quotations, or passages that capture a particular moment or feeling, really adds to the personal feel of a wedding, and helps to share our emotions, particularly if we can't find a way to express it in our own words. Readings can also be used to illustrate a particular point or theme, and they can add humour.

However, couples often tell me that finding the right readings is one of the most overwhelming parts of preparing for their ceremony. There is simply so much choice: traditional poetry; readings from the Bible; Shakespeare; a piece of prose; the lyrics of a favourite song; the speech from a favourite film; contemporary writers; sacred texts; pieces written specially for the occasion – the list seems endless. The internet is an amazing resource, but in the case of finding readings for your wedding it often throws up far too much material, and instead of finding inspiration we can feel swamped. So for that reason I am not going to offer a long list of possible readings. I have used some sections to illustrate particular points, but it is more important that, whether you want something light-hearted, serious or romantic, you choose a wedding reading that best reflects your relationship and type of ceremony.

The search for something personal is an opportunity for you and your spouse-to-be to talk about the meanings of both your relationship and your ceremony. Most importantly, have fun discovering which readings are most meaningful to you and your fiancé/e, and why it can turn out to be one of the most insightful wedding preparations you do together.

What is possible?

Depending on the type of ceremony you are having, there may be limits on what is permitted. If you are having a religious service, then your minister, pastor, priest, or celebrant will probably have some suggestions to guide you, and you may be surprised by how many options there are for readings, prayers, and blessings. Some civil ceremonies and some humanist ceremonies will not permit any religious readings at all, and then your choice is from the vast range of secular writings. Or you may be fortunate enough to be planning a ceremony where you have freedom to include materials from any source, religious or non-religious; certainly, that is what I can offer to the couples who I marry in Scotland. Including readings in your ceremony gives you the opportunity to reflect on your own unique relationship and your future as a married couple.

Some couples choose readings which display the depth and intimacy of their relationship, while others prefer more privacy and want to have wedding readings that talk about more general themes of love and marriage. Others may think it important to make their guests laugh, and some like to ensure that all beliefs are acknowledged and welcomed so may include readings from a variety of religious or sacred texts.

Kit and Maria did not have a strong faith or belief but they appreciated the wisdom in the Bible. During their wedding, they wanted to honour Maria's mother's own faith and her desire to reflect something of that without alienating the many atheist guests. Maria's mother spoke about love being patient and kind, and how it always protects, always trusts, always hopes, always perseveres (extracts from 1 Corinthians, chapter 13), and concluded with advice from Philippians chapter 4 to think about whatever is true, noble, right, and pure.

Finding the perfect readings

Whether you are searching for something thoughtful, romantic, funny, modern or traditional, use a variety of sources to look for inspiration. You may want to read through the library of wedding readings found online, or buy a specialist book which contains lots of examples and options, but don't feel limited or constrained by published selections. Look for inspiration everywhere – watching movies, listening to music, or reading books – you might be surprised by where you find a passage that really speaks to you.

My first suggestion when you are starting to look for your wedding readings, is to enlist the help of those who know you best. You don't want them to come up with 40 pages of readings taken from the internet, you want them to delve into shared memories. Perhaps your parents recall the readings they had at their wedding; perhaps a grandmother has a book of poetry that she used to read to you when you were a child; maybe a friend will remind you about a favourite author. Even chatting about the subject with friends may give you some inspiration for where to look. Emily had a letter written by her great-grandmother to her great-grandfather while he was working on a tea plantation in India. You may not be fortunate enough to have a unique piece of history like this, but you might find similar ideas in a published book of letters written during the time of the world wars.

When Mike and Jenni were getting married, Mike's mum reminded him about a poem that he had written when he was young. It is easy to slip into the stereotypical thinking which assumes that girls have been dreaming about their wedding since they were young, but when Mike was age 12 and a pupil at Junior School, he had his writing published in a compilation of poems by children across the region. We read it during their wedding, immediately before the pronouncement:

The Wedding, by Michael Law, age 12
I stand at the end of a pew,
In the fear that she, my only love,
Is having second thoughts.
I tremble as the doors open

And then I relax as she enters.
The organ starts. It's my big moment.
She stands beside me, my future wife.
All that's between us now are the
most important words I could ever hear:
'I now pronounce you man and wife.'

And then I did indeed pronounce Mike and Jenni as husband and wife ☺ [reproduced with permission of Michael Law, now age 32].

If your wedding has a particular theme or is being held in a particular season, that can be a good place to start. For example, exploring the writings of John Muir if the wedding is out of doors and the wedding couple are interested in nature; something by Mark Twain for a vintage American theme; or beach-themed readings such as Somewhere, by Linda Harnett, which speaks of being on a beach together, or I Would Live in Your Love, by Sara Teasdale, which likens love to waves on the sea.

You may have some favourite authors or movies, and the internet can throw up some incredible finds and help you to find something different and unique which is meaningful to the two of you. In ceremonies I've held, I have included readings from Dr Zhivago by Boris Pasternak, as well as poems by Charlotte Brontë, Victor Hugo, Bob Marley, Neil Gaiman, and many others.

Of course, many weddings include classics from literature, readings from the Bible, Shakespeare sonnets, and also popular contemporary readings such as The One by Cheryl J Barclay, or the passage about tree roots being entwined, taken from Captain Corelli's Mandolin by Louis de Bernières.

Don't worry if the reading you have chosen is the same one as a friend used in their ceremony, and don't be concerned that your guests will have heard it all before. There's a reason why popular readings become popular – because they're appropriate, and the words and sentiments are beautiful. Even if you or your guests have been to several other weddings that also used these popular choices, in the context and setting of YOUR wedding, it will have meaning for you, and people will sense that, and enjoy it.

Using song lyrics

You or your fiancé(e) may have a song that you love so much it makes you cry; one that exactly describes your relationship, including all the difficult parts. It may be that 'your song', while meaningful and important, is not one that you could use for your first dance – it may be impossible to dance to, or it may not suit the mood of your reception – so including it as a reading is a wonderful way of sharing the depth of your friendship and love, or even celebrating the light-hearted and humorous times that you enjoy.

Naturally, song lyrics in particular have a lot of repetition in them, the repetition of a chorus, or a particular line or phrase used several times at the end of each verse, so you may want to make some modifications to how much of it you use. This leads to a big question: do you need to stick with the original version of a poem or text, or can you amend or paraphrase so that the words suit you and your situation better?

My personal opinion on this is that if you are using a religious passage or if you are quoting from a well-known piece of writing, such as Shakespeare or Robert Burns, then you should stick with the original. To use words from a religious text and then alter them, may find you applying them out of context; changing the words of a famous poem may have some of your guests wondering about the accuracy, and may even infringe copyright laws. However, adjusting a well-known piece of writing can work well if you make it clear that this is what is being done.

When Chris and Karen were married, they based their vows on Rudyard Kipling's poem, If. The adaptations they made were so clear and personal that it was obvious they had used the poem as inspiration, and had not simply missed out a couple of words. This is the conclusion of their vows:

If we can lift each other when we need

If we can work together to achieve our goals

If we can share our family and our lives,

Then I will marry you (spoken by Chris)

And I will marry you (spoken by Karen)

And we will have a strong, happy, and lasting marriage. (spoken by Chris and Karen together)

There are some lovely passages of prose which are quite long. For example, Laurie Lee's *Essay on Love*, Bob Marley's writing which begins "Only once in your life, you find someone who can turn your world around...", or *The Art of Marriage by Wilfred A Peterson*. You may not want to have these read in their entirety, but instead to choose abridged versions which contain the words, stanzas, or lines which are particularly relevant to you. Make it clear that what you are reading is an extract or abridged version, or ask your celebrant to do this when they introduce the reading.

Readings can also be an opportunity to introduce and reflect someone or somethings important that cannot be included in your wedding physically. Sometimes a reading might reflect the couple's love of adventure, for example, Dr Seuss's Oh the Places You'll Go, or it might reflect a much loved pet who has been left in peace at home for the day, for example, Why Falling in Love is Like Owning a Dog, or other similar pieces.

When Nicola and Calum got married, Nicola's brother Kenneth was in Canada. His wife had given birth three days before the wedding, and it was impossible for them to attend. Kenneth had chosen a reading which another family member read, and which echoed Kenneth's wishes for Calum and Nicola and their future – for strength to shelter love through difficult times, to protect love against adversity, and for love to be a guiding star for the couple throughout their married life.

Some couples offer their readers a short list from which to choose, or simply ask *them* to choose the wedding readings. If your readers are close friends and family whose judgement you trust, you may enjoy the surprise of not knowing what the reading will be and appreciate experiencing it along with your guests on the big day. Of course, this approach carries some risk. You don't know quite what they'll choose or if it will reflect your taste or values, so you may want to offer some guidelines – even if it is only on length, and your desire not to offend any guests.

How many readings?

Typically, most ceremonies have between one and three readings. These may be spaced out: one linked to the words of welcome and opening to help set the tone of the ceremony; one linked to the story of the couple's relationship, to reflect something personal or illustrate an important aspect of their love; or maybe immediately before the vows, to emphasise the commitment the couple are about to make. *Union*, by Robert Fulghum, is particularly apt at this point. You might also like to include a reading at the closing point of the ceremony – something that offers good wishes for the couple's future, or which is a blessing.

Ultimately, there are no hard and fast rules about the number of readings – and, of course, you don't need to include any. Often the readings are placed throughout the ceremony, but at one wedding I held, all five bridesmaids wanted to read. We found five short readings which together told a story: one about the bride's love for the groom; one about the groom's love for the bride; one about adventures and travel; one about the promises made on the wedding day; and one with blessings for the future. It made sense for the readings all to come in one place, and to be linked with a few lines of narrative.

If you have found many pieces that you love but too many to include in your ceremony, let your celebrant know about all the words you like, not just the final readings you have chosen, and perhaps they can incorporate some lines from them into other parts of the ceremony. Alternatively, you could include favourite quotations in your order of service, use them to decorate your tables for dinner, or incorporate them into your speeches and toasts.

Whatever you choose for your readings, and however many, ask your celebrant to link them into your ceremony – tell them who is reading and why, and what is important about the piece so they can give it context and ensure that your guests understand the meaning. This is particularly important if you have chosen something unusual or quirky. Bill and Veronica's choice of *The Love Monkey* made sense and was delightful once everyone knew that they were both zoologists and that their first date was to a monkey sanctuary. By contrast, I was a guest at a wedding where there was a reading from the children's book, *The Velveteen Rabbit*. It is an allegorical tale about human love, but the selected passage was read without context. It was unclear how the reading fitted into the rest of the ceremony, and I know that some of the guests were left feeling rather puzzled.

Who is Giving the Wedding Reading?

This may be one of your biggest considerations. It can be lovely to have someone read who is not already involved in the ceremony – maybe a family member, or friend who couldn't be a bridesmaid, or perhaps making sure that there is someone from both the bride and groom's family reading. However, it is important to make sure the person you ask is comfortable, and confident, and also that their personal style suits the reading you have chosen. It is a disappointment to have spent ages choosing a reading carefully and thoughtfully, only to find that the speaker is very quiet or nervous and that no-one can hear them properly, or to have chosen something light-hearted, fun and mischievous, and have it read in a dreary, monotonous tone.

Sometimes people who are not used to speaking in public get very anxious when they think about reading at a wedding. So it can be better to find a friend or family member who can speak loudly, slowly, and clearly, and who is not likely to be too overwhelmed by the emotion of the moment. I find that the mothers of the couple who are getting married, or the children of the bride and groom, are the most likely to find themselves feeling a little overwhelmed, even when they are used to speaking in front of groups. Michelle's mum was a teacher and used to dealing with a large class of noisy pupils, but she was surprised by how difficult it was to read at her daughter's wedding. She told me afterwards, 'I had chosen a reading which seemed so perfect for Michelle and Sean, and it included references to parents and children. Then suddenly at the wedding, the words reminded me of my own father who had died several years earlier, and I really struggled to stand up and speak. I hadn't expected anything like that to happen and I wish I'd asked my sister, Michelle's aunt, to be prepared to read as a back-up.'

Of course, a few tears and someone being a bit choked up are all fine and add to the depth of feeling on the day, but you don't want your readers to be so emotional or anxious that they feel awful during your ceremony, or to imagine that they've spoiled things for you if they have to break off for a moment or two. If there was a scale of emotion from 1 to 10 (where 1 is low emotion or apathy and 10 is extreme anxiety or high emotion), then you probably want your readers to be in the 4-5 range at the start, which allows for a slight increase in emotions during the reading without the reader, and the couple, falling apart mid-ceremony.

You will be fortunate indeed, if the person who is reading at your wedding is a natural storyteller, performer, and raconteur. Most often, you are relying on friends and family members who are not comfortable with speaking in public, so you will want to make things as enjoyable, and as easy as possible for them.

Practicalities

Your venue may have a sound system and microphones which make it easier for your readers to be heard; make sure you check this out beforehand. If you are having a video made, your videographers may ask that people doing the readings use a small microphone clipped to their lapel so that the words can be captured on the soundtrack.

On a very practical note, think about what your readers are going to read from. The reading printed on card is always going to look smarter than someone pulling a piece of folded-up paper from their pocket, and on a personal basis I hate to rely on technology. It can quite spoil the moment for a couple if their reader comes up and then spends several minutes scrolling through their phone to find the reading, or finds that they need an internet connection in order to pull up the text.

As a celebrant, I ask for a copy of the readings which I always have with me as part of my ceremony booklet. If the reading is a surprise for you as a couple, I request that the people reading send me a copy of what they will read. This means that I can make the right kind of introduction, so I'm not making a deadly serious introduction to a light-hearted humorous piece, or vice versa. It also means that if a reader has forgotten their card or notes (and you'd be surprised by how often that happens), then I can easily provide them with a copy. If one of your bridesmaids is reading, then she probably won't want to walk down the aisle clutching a piece of paper, so have copies available at the venue beforehand. Also, don't forget to print the reading in a large font so that no-one has to peer at tiny script, or ask to borrow spectacles.

Whether or not a couple are having a rehearsal, I always encourage the people who are reading to rehearse and to practise. It is one thing to read through a poem or piece of prose silently, and it is quite another to stand up and project your voice to 100 people or more. These are my five top tips for readers at a wedding:

1. Have the readings available in plenty of time, at least three or four weeks before the wedding;

2. Rehearse by speaking out loud – several times. Your mouth will become accustomed to the words and their rhythm, so that it flows more naturally;

3. During the ceremony, sit close to the aisle so that you can get out of your seat easily without having to clamber over other guests, and when you get to the front, walk behind the groom rather than the bride, to avoid standing on her dress;

4. Take everything slowly: pause before you start (and breathe); make a deliberate pause at the end of lines or verses – full stops, commas and paragraphs are there for a reason (and remember to breathe); and if the reading contains humour, make sure you allow sufficient time for people to register the funny moments, and to laugh.

5. Look at the bride and groom. Of course you want
   everyone else to hear the reading, but essentially
   this is a special message for the couple getting
   married, so direct the reading at them, and smile,
   and be happy (and don't forget to breathe).

You may want to have a copy of your reading on your
order of service, if you're having one, so that all your
guests know what the reading is and have a memento to
take away with them. Please be careful about copyright,
though. Some commercial printers will not print a reading on an order of service or ceremony programme, if you
do not have copyright permission.

Depending on who you have asked to read, different
selections may be more or less appropriate. Don't ask the
most serious friend you have to read a humorous poem –
it will need someone with a sense of comic timing. And if
you've chosen poetry, make sure your reader is comfortable finding where to pause and where to give emphasis.
Readings which offer advice may best be read by a parent
or older sibling or relative, and readings from children's
books can be very effective if they are offered by someone
younger. Then there are some things which often don't
work well at all. At one wedding, the bride's godfather
– who lived in London and had a Cockney accent – had
been asked to recite a poem by the Scottish writer, Robert
Burns. He did so in a fake Scots accent, and most of the
guests looked horrified!

It can be interesting to have a pair of readers offering
relevant sections. For example, the Edward Monkton
book, *A Lovely Love Story*, can be more effective if it is
read by one male and one female for appropriate sections,
rather than being read all by one person. At a wedding

recently, the two readers were given copies of the 1930s book *How to Be a Good Wife* and the companion book *How to Be a Good Husband*. In a light-hearted, tongue-in-cheek manner, the best man and chief bridesmaid, who both knew the couple well, lifted sections from this old-fashioned and rather unpopular advice and applied it to the couple getting married, reflecting both their strengths and foibles in a way which was clever and very funny.

As groom and bride, you may want to read to each other – either poems or readings which each of you has selected, or perhaps alternate verses of a poem such as *Love* by Roy Croft, or alternate verses of *The Colour of my Love* sung by Celine Dion.

Using Quotations during the Ceremony

Readings do not have to be given in isolation. One of the loveliest ways for me to construct a ceremony is when a couple give me several readings, song lyrics, or quotations that they love, and I can weave them into relevant sections of the ceremony – perhaps something to open the ceremony, such as these words from Mark Twain for the opening of Chris and Karen's ceremony: '*Life is short, Break the Rules. Forgive quickly, Kiss SLOWLY. Love truly. Laugh uncontrollably. And never regret ANYTHING that makes you smile.*' Or an extract from the book *Clockwork Prince*, for Vi and Ronnie, who loved the *Infernal Devices* trilogy.

Sharon and Craig had a Scottish-themed wedding and their personal section included quotations from Sean Connery, Robert Louis Stevenson, Sir Walter Scott: 'Love rules the courts, the camp, the grove, And men below, and saints above: For love is heaven, and heaven is love.' Robert Burns: 'To see her was to love her, to love only her, and to love her forever.' Also from William Wallace, and even the comic character, Oor Wullie.

Readings as Closing Blessings or Benedictions

There are some readings which work particularly well at the end of a ceremony – almost like a blessing, to wish the couple well on their way, and to offer everyone's best wishes for their future. Well known readings include the *Apache Blessing,* one of the varieties of the Celtic Prayer, or an adaptation of Mark Twain's work putting the words into the future tense: *'May marriage make your two fractional lives a whole, …may it give a new gladness to the sunshine, a new fragrance to the flowers, a new beauty to the earth, and a new mystery to life.'*

A few of my favourites

Perhaps you are very fortunate and someone close to you will have written their own poem or prose, something which really summarises your feelings and touches your hearts. But if not, then here are a few of my favourite readings:

Why marriage? **by Mari Nichols-Haining**

For Now **by Tracey Emin**

The Wedding Poem **by Neil Gaiman, written for his friend's wedding**

From *Les Misérables* **by Victor Hugo:** *'The future belongs to hearts even more than it does to minds. Love,* *that is the only thing that can occupy and fill eternity. In the infinite, the inexhaustible is requisite.*

Love participates of the soul itself. It is of the same nature. Like it, it is the divine spark; like it, it is incorruptible, indivisible, imperishable. It is a point of fire that exists within us, which is immortal and infinite, which nothing can confine, and which nothing can extinguish. We feel it burning even to the very marrow of our bones, and we see it beaming in the very depths of heaven.'

Kiera Cass – *The One*

The writing by Mary Ann Shaffer, about the hero and the heroine

From *Jane Eyre* by Charlotte Brontë: *'I have for the first time found what I can truly love – I have found you. You are my sympathy — my better self — my good angel — I am bound to you with a strong attachment. I think you good, gifted, lovely: a fervent, a solemn passion is conceived in my heart; it leans to you, draws you to my centre and spring of life, wrap my existence about you — and, kindling in pure, powerful flame, fuses you and me in one.'*

From *First Poems* by Rainer Maria Rilke

Understand, I'll slip quietly
Away from the noisy crowd
When I see the pale
Stars rising, blooming over the oaks.
I'll pursue solitary pathways
Through the pale twilit meadows,
With only this one dream:
You come too.

Extracts from *Dr Zhivago* by Boris Pasternak

Extracts from Goodridge v. Dept. of Public Health *(the case that legalised gay marriage in Massachusetts):*

What do YOU want?

- Favourite poems or books:

- Favourite authors and poets:

- Favourite song lyrics:

- What type of reading suits the style of our wedding?

- Who would like to read? Who would we like to read?

Chapter 8: Symbolic Gestures and Rituals

A marriage ceremony is a complex and delightful mix of tangible and intangible elements: tangible in that the couple and their guests are physically present at a particular location, and there is legal documentation to be signed. Usually there is a particular outfit to be worn, flowers, food, and much, much more. Yet the promises and vows that a bride and groom make to each other encapsulate words, feelings, and sentiments which are not visible and which, on the wedding day, may pass all too quickly – even if recorded and watched later on video.

Symbolic gestures are an opportunity to represent the deepest of emotions in a physical form, and thereby to focus and elaborate on its meaning. In Western cultures and many others, the most frequently used symbolic gesture is the exchange of rings – a visible reminder of the commitments and promise of marriage – and this has been described in a previous chapter.

Gestures and ritual can also be part of tradition, whether that is drawn from culture, religion, heritage, belief or folklore. They can be a way of linking two different backgrounds or concepts together, or they can create something new that is unique to the couple getting married – you can really let your imagination flourish here. ☺ The most important rule is to be clear about what you are trying to represent, and then to choose or create the gesture or ritual which is most important and relevant.

There are four main sentiments which are expressed frequently in wedding ceremonies:

- Unity: the joining of two individuals into one life together.

- Commitment: the lifelong bond that is the intention of the couple.

- Trust and sharing: commitment to be there together in good times and bad.

- Love and protection: the celebration of the heart of a relationship.

The examples in the rest of this chapter offer simple rituals involving the couple, but each of these can be expanded to include others who are important in your ceremony. This, and other ways of involving your guests, is covered in Chapter 9. I have also included in this chapter some ways of including individual symbolic expressions or family traditions, and a few examples which have their origins in different religions, traditions or cultures.

Section 1: UNITY RITUALS

(see appendix 1 for sample wording)

Gestures to represent unity recognise that a marriage celebrates the joining of two people – mature individuals, each with their own personality, upbringing, character, personal history, and preferences in the way they communicate. Yet, in getting married, two people are making a commitment to be united and to journey through life together, somehow adapting to and accepting the delights and challenges posed by two different people creating a long-lasting relationship.

The two most frequently used elements are unity candles and unity sand.

Unity Candle

At its most simple, this gesture has a candle or flames representing each person and all the individuality, characteristics, and love that they each bring to the relationship and their marriage. Each individual person is beautiful and whole in their own right, but when they choose to join in marriage, they create something new and unique between themselves – so the couple use the two candle flames together to light one unity candle, symbolic of their life together.

Some couples choose to extinguish their individual flames after the unity flame is lit, demonstrating the irrevocable nature of the commitment they're making. Others choose to keep all three candles lit, showing the harmonious presence and importance of both individuality and unity.

A unity candle can be something for you to keep and to relight on special occasions, such as anniversaries, or whenever you have negotiated the tricky balance between individual wants and needs and the shared compromise of marriage.

If you are using candles in your ceremony, there are some practicalities to consider, including safety – my colleague tells of the horror of seeing a bride's veil catch light, but fortunately extinguished before any real damage was done. I often have a small tea-light already lit on the table or altar to avoid messing around with matches or lighters during the ceremony, and I bring long wax tapers so that candles placed inside deep glass holders can be lit easily, without the risk of burnt fingers or dripping wax.

Mike and Kayleigh loved the concept of the unity candle ceremony, however they were getting married in Mike's parents' garden, on what they hoped would be a sunny day! Kayleigh worried that the impact of candlelight might be lost, and of course there was the practical problem of the wind blowing the candles out.

Unity Sand

Mike and Kayleigh (and many others) opted for a sand ritual. Using the same concept as the unity candle, there is sand representing the groom and sand representing the bride – symbolising each of them as individuals. Each person pours half their sand into the unity sand jar or vase, showing all their unique qualities, and then the couple pour their remaining sand in together. As the sand is poured together, the grains of sand mix, forming a beautiful new pattern and depicting how the lives of the couple are now inseparable.

You can buy unity sand and vases online – there are many colours of sand, and some couples also choose to have the unity sand vase engraved with their names, their wedding date, and maybe a special message. The different colours of sand may represent particular characteristics – e.g. red for warmth and passion, yellow for harmony, etc. A list of symbolic colours is provided later in this chapter.

An alternative is to use sand from particular locations – a beach you like to visit, or from your home town or country, for example. However, please be cautious if you intend bringing sand from a different country; environmental legislation has some pretty strict rules about transporting soil through customs!

Adam and Bronwyn had their ceremony on a little beach on a Scottish island. The sun shone all day, and their two children spent the morning building sandcastles and collecting shells. During the ceremony, Bronwyn and Adam layered sand into a jar: a base layer for their appreciation of earth, nature, and everything that grows on the land and sea; a layer for each of them; a layer for their children and family life; and finally a layer showing their commitment to their marriage and depicting how their love would protect their family, sustain their individuality, and encourage them in their wish to live in a way which is kind to the environment.

During the ceremony, the children continued adding to the sand jar, with seashells and buckets of sea water, bringing their own playful influence to bear on the proceedings. I doubt that the jar of murky sand and water will ever have pride of place on a mantelpiece, but it was a beautiful example of a family creating something together, and there were lots of photos taken to help jog memories of that day.

Each couple has their own preference for sand ceremony containers, which may be elegant or rustic. You'll need three containers: one each to hold the sand that you will pour, and a vessel for you to pour your sand into. If you want to have a keepsake or memento, then choose a receptacle with a lid or seal for the top. Be as creative as you want in decorating your sand receptacle, and let it reflect your character and the style of the wedding.

With the exception of the beach example from Adam and Bronwyn's wedding, it is important that the sand is dry, in order to pour well, and also to be something you can keep.

Creative Alternatives

Building on the concept of the sand ceremony, it is possible to buy an hourglass set. You each put your sand inside and seal the container. Every time the hourglass is turned upside down, the grains of sand mix more, showing how the couple become more and more entwined with every passing year. You could agree to tip the hourglass on your anniversary and notice how much more your lives have mixed together.

Instead of using candles or sand, you could use your favourite drinks to create a special cocktail, or exploit the alchemy of coloured liquids. There is a frequently watched clip on the internet, when a couple add two clear liquids together and watch as they change colour.

I have held ceremonies for two people who were bakers, who added the ingredients for a cake – it was then baked and served to guests later in the day – and I also created a salt ceremony for a couple where the groom's family name was Salt.

Appendix 1 at the end of this book includes examples of some of the words which could be used in a simple unity candle ceremony, unity sand ceremony, cake ceremony, or salt ceremony.

Section 2: GESTURES OF COMMITMENT (including handfasting)

(see appendix 1 for sample wording)

Gestures of commitment are most frequently symbolised by the tying of ribbons or cords, for example, creating a fisherman's knot, tying a Celtic knot, incorporating a Mexican 'Lazo', or performing a handfasting. They represent that your lives are bound firmly together and that your lives are entwined. Each of these gestures are emblematic of the phrase 'Tying the knot', and many different traditions claim themselves to be the origin of this saying.

In a fisherman's knot, the couple use two cords to tie a knot which becomes stronger and tighter over time – and the harder you pull on it, the stronger the tie becomes. A Celtic knot represents the interweaving aspects of life and it often depicts three elements, e.g. love, laughter, and life; or past, present, and future.

During a handfasting, the couple's clasped hands are gently bound with ribbon or fabric. The binding of hands during a marriage ceremony is found in many cultures throughout the ages and in many parts of the world, including handfastings which have pagan roots and those of Celtic origin.

Celtic handfastings have become particularly popular in recent years – those of you who have seen the film *Braveheart* may have glimpsed that in the marriage scene between William Wallace and his bride Murron their hands are tied. This type of handfasting can be done with one cord, two cords, or many cords.

If you choose one cord it represents that, although there are two of you getting married, there is one love that binds you and commits you to each other. If you use two cords it often represents the joining of two individuals and also two families or clans – especially if you use a family tartan or other material. These can be wrapped around your hands in such a way that, when the couple draw their hands apart, the two ribbons or cords are tied together in a knot. There are several different ways in which to tie a 'magic knot', so be sure to check with your celebrant or officiant and maybe to practise how it is done. Multiple ribbons can represent the important elements in your marriage, e.g. past, present, and future, or you could use one ribbon for each important value in your relationship, e.g. trust, equality, sense of humour, communication, and love (this would require five ribbons).

Different colours of ribbon can represent different attributes in your relationship:

Red: passion, strength, lust, fertility

Orange: encouragement, attraction, kindness, plenty

Yellow: charm, confidence, joy, balance

Green: prosperity, fertility, charity, health

Blue: tranquillity, patience, devotion, sincerity

Purple: power, devotion, goodness, tenderness

Black: strength, wisdom, vision, success

White: purity, concentration, meditation, peace

Grey: neutrality, balance, compromise, harmony

Pink: unity, honour, truth, romance, happiness

Brown: earth, grounding, talent, home

Silver: treasure, values, creativity, inspiration

Gold: energy, wealth, intelligence, longevity

To help your guests understand the significance of your ritual, it is important that your celebrant explains what is happening and what the ribbons and the handfasting symbolise.

To make a handfasting practical, the couple's bound hands must at some time be untied. I most often do this without untying any knots which have been made, but I usually like to remind everyone that the tying of the knot is symbolic and that what actually binds the couple is their love for each other and the promises they have made in their marriage vows. A handfasting can be integrated into the ceremony so the bride and groom make their vows to one another while their hands are bound, then remove the ties before they exchange rings.

To perform a handfasting, the couple can stand side by side facing in the same direction, with their lower arms next to each other (parallel from the elbow to the wrist), and with the right arm of one partner bound to the left arm of the other. Alternatively, the couple can face each other and clasp right hand to right hand (although holding the wrist gives a firmer grip than holding the hand). This leaves one hand tied, and one hand free – helpful if you need to scratch an itchy nose or wipe a tear from your eye. A third option is one in which the couple face each other, clasp right hand to right hand AND left hand to left hand, so that between you, you are making a figure of eight, or an infinity symbol representing infinite, unending love.

Creative Alternatives

There are some other lovely ways to symbolise a binding commitment. Many people are familiar with the concept of attaching a 'love lock' to a bridge, and using **locks and keys** is a lovely way to demonstrate the intention that your commitment is long-lasting, and also that the key is given only to the two people involved.

Marty and Sylvia held their ceremony in a spectacular beauty spot adjacent to a wild waterfall. During the wedding, they placed a copy of their marriage vows into a carved wooden box, attached a lock and then threw the key into the deep river, showing that they were locked for all time into the joint vows and promises that they had made to each other.

Hannah and Bing included a ring warming in their ceremony. The wedding rings were looped onto a padlock which was locked with two keys, before the rings and lock were passed around all the guests. At the point in the ceremony when the rings were to be exchanged, Bing gave Hannah one of the keys, and Hannah gave Bing the other key. They exchanged rings with the following words: 'I give you this ring, and with it I give you the key to my heart. Our marriage is the magical process which unlocks my love for you for all time.'

I have also held ceremonies where the couples have created a wedding time-capsule, or a box containing love letters or a bottle of wine, and then wrapped a chain around the box, padlocked it, and put the key in a place for safe keeping until a future day when the box would be opened.

Often, alongside a lock and key ritual, a wedding ceremony might include a relevant reading such as *The Key to My Heart* by Nicole C Moore, or an extract from *The Bridge Across Forever* by Richard Bach. Perhaps these symbolic gestures and others involving keys and padlocks are linked to the word 'wedlock'! Although historically the word comes from wed meaning pledge, and lac/loc meaning action, i.e. pledge giving or pledge making.

Other traditional ways of symbolising a permanent commitment are with the use of an **Oathing Stone**. For hundreds of years, making a pledge over a stone has symbolised the making of an unbreakable promise; from the 13th Century, carving or etching a promise into stone was seen as a way in which to make a binding contract. In Scottish traditions, the bride and groom place their hands upon a stone while saying their wedding vows as a way of expressing their solemn promises in a physical form.

In most modern weddings, the couple use a stone which can be held in their hands or placed on a table, and some couples choose to have the stone engraved with their names and wedding date as a permanent keepsake. Sometimes there are smaller stones made of the same minerals for the guests to hold during the ceremony. These are then returned after the ceremony to show the support of family and friends, and to remind the bride and groom of the love and support that surrounds them in their marriage.

Chris and Julie were married next to a Scottish loch (lake).
They spent some days before the wedding building a cairn
tower from large rocks, stones, and pebbles, and they had
chosen one particular stone as their oathing stone. The
tower of rocks was symbolic of all the events in their lives
and the foundation of their relationship, and at the start of
the ceremony they invited their guests to add to the cairn,
offering their blessings and good wishes for Julie and Chris
and their marriage. They made their vows with their right
hands placed on the oathing stone, asking their guests and
all of nature to bear witness to their pledges. After the
ceremony, the oathing stone was carried inside to have place
of honour during the ensuing celebrations, and the following
day Chris and Julie returned it to the shore to be washed by
the waters of the loch for the rest of their lifetime.

Appendix 1 at the end of this book includes examples
of some of the words which could be used in a knot tying
ceremony, handfasting, or oathing stone.

Section 3: GESTURES OF TRUST AND SHARING

(see appendix 1 for sample wording)

The suggestions in this section are symbolic of practical
support and commitment, and they often involve foods,
drink, money or treasures.

In a pagan handfasting, for example, there is often inclusion of a shared drink and food (usually oats) with
the guests, as part of the actual ceremony.

In Alan and Kaia's wedding, they stood around a fire and
shared flapjacks and a drink of honey mead. 'You stand

before the fire. The fire is lit to burn up and destroy anything of harm. A fire offers warmth and protection... And round the fire we have food and drink to celebrate good fortune, to acknowledge the good things we bring from last year, and to share amongst friends and family. So as Alan and Kaia seal their union, they step forward into a joint future, with the protective powers of the fire, and the sharing of abundance.'

There are several other examples of the couple **sharing a drink,** either from a loving cup, or in Celtic traditions from a flat two-handled bowl called a quaich. Sharing a drink from the same cup is symbolic of the trust that both partners have in each other. It is an old Scottish story that when two clans or families met together, the clan chiefs would share a drink from the quaich. The gesture showed that the two parties had only the best intentions for each other and intended no harm. Because the cup was offered and received with both hands, it proved that no dagger was being held, and because the chiefs drank from the same bowl, it showed that no poison had been added to the liquid! As a wedding ritual, sharing a drink in this way represents the commitment that each person makes to do no harm to the other, and the trust of each partner in accepting that.

Sharing a drink is also symbolic of the couple's intention to share everything together. Fill the cup with a drink which has both sweet properties and bitter properties. This could be lemonade with a squeeze of lemon in it, or a glass of wine, or whisky – in fact, most alcoholic drinks contain both sweet and bitter elements. This is a metaphor for the couple's commitment to share everything that life brings to them in the future – the good things, and the more difficult things.

In addition to the symbolism of sharing a drink, there can also be meaning in what you choose to drink. Ian and Pam were married late in the evening and they shared a pot of tea – reviving, refreshing, and full of warmth and sweetness, while many couples choose a glass of wine. A glass of wine, like a marriage, is the consequence of many years of work and patience – the nurturing of the vine, the tender care of the growing grapes, the blending of ingredients, the waiting for fermentation, and the developing flavours with each passing year.

Eleanor and Ralph wanted to show their willingness to share all the good and bad that life might bring them, and they did this by tasting four ingredients – salt, sour, bitter and sweet. There were four bowls prepared before the wedding, and during the ceremony they dipped their fingers into each in turn and placed a small amount of the liquid on each other's tongue. They shared drops of salt water in anticipation of life's tears and sadness; they shared drops of lemon juice in anticipation of any times when their relationship was soured and they felt disillusioned or regretful; they shared drops of tonic water in anticipation of the potential bitterness of conflict or disagreement; and they shared drops of honey showing the shared commitment to the sweetness of their love. Ralph and Eleanor also included a fifth dish representing Umami – a savoury which balances the taste and rounds out the overall flavour of a dish, and enhances the palatability of a wide variety of foods. We compared this to their marriage: 'the unknown mystery that takes the everyday elements of life and makes something magical.'

Sharing food or cakes

There are many different ideas if the bride and groom want to symbolise their relationship by sharing food. In some Eastern European cultures, the mothers of the bride and groom bring forward a loaf of bread which the couple rip apart and eat. This symbolises that the parents' role in feeding and supporting their children has come to an end and the married couple are now responsible for their own living, and it also represents the blessing from the families and their hope that the newlyweds will never go hungry.

When Sree and Han were married, they ended the ceremony by eating from a plate of nuts, dates, pomegranate, and rice, symbolising good health, sweetness and happiness, fertility, and prosperity.

When guests arrived at Steven and Linda's wedding ceremony, they were surprised to find the wedding cake in pride of place when they entered the ceremony room. Linda's aunt had made the cake and decorated it, and Steven and Linda wanted to show their appreciation by including it in the ceremony; they also wanted to use the cake as a way of reflecting the important aspects of their relationship. The symbolism included – dried fruits for richness and delight; sugar for sweet moments; almonds for long life; flour and eggs for appreciation of the everyday things which bind all the sweet moments together; and white icing for beauty, purity and faithfulness. The three layers represented the couple's past, present, and future (and yes, they did keep the top layer to celebrate the birth of their baby). Cutting the cake was the first act that Linda and Steven did together as a married couple, and then they fed each other small pieces of cake to show their commitment to provide and care for each other.

Giving Coins

The giving of gold or silver coins during a wedding ceremony is seen in many cultures across the world. There are several possible meanings:

- Wishes for good luck and good fortune

- Hope or prosperity

- A commitment from the groom to the bride, and from the bride to the groom, to always work hard and provide for their future

- A promise from both the bride and groom for responsible stewardship – taking good care of everything that the couple value

- A commitment to share everything they own with each other

- Blessings for every month of the year (and one extra for the hard times or the honeymoon)

- Appreciation of the thirteen values of marriage – love, peace, commitment, trust, respect, joy, happiness, nurturing, honesty, harmony, wholeness, faithfulness, and cooperation.

This ritual originated in Spain, and is popular in Mexico and throughout Latin America. Usually the celebrant calls for the box of coins towards the end of the ceremony, after the vows have been made. The coins are then passed from the groom to the bride and then from the bride to the groom, sometimes several times between them. If the coins represent the thirteen virtues, then your officiant or celebrant may read the list as the coins are transferred one by one between the couple.

Alternatives

Julie and Ken were young and light-hearted. The friends at their wedding were part of a big group of pals who often went out together and had a lot of fun. Ken and Julie were an integral part of the group and, despite their four-year relationship and their strong love for each other, they rarely displayed their affection in public. Of course, during their marriage they spoke about their love and the bond that they had, but they would have felt very uncomfortable (as would their friends) if the ceremony was too soppy or sentimental. In the weeks leading up to the wedding, Julie and Ken agreed that they wanted to find a way to share their deepest promises and emotions with each other, so they each chose to write a love letter. They didn't share these immediately, and during their wedding ceremony they placed them into a box, along with a bottle of wine. They agreed that on the anniversary of their wedding they would open the box, drink the wine, and share their letters with each other.

Interestingly, a few weeks after their first anniversary, Ken and Julie came back to me. They had each been overwhelmed by the tenderness and the thoughtfulness of the letter the other person had written, and they wanted to renew their vows using a few of the lines from their love letters.

Along similar lines, a treasure box is popular in wedding ceremonies. During the ceremony, the couple place into a box some treasures which would remind them of their wedding day, their happiness and joy, and their love. This might be a copy of their vows, or a love letter or other memento, with the treasure box being opened on their wedding anniversary or other occasion. Sometimes key guests, such as parents or godparents, are involved in the ritual, adding something of significance for the couple, either a gift added as a treat for when the box is opened, or an item that conveys advice or a poignant reminder. I have seen treasure boxes which contain wine, whisky, money, candles, poems, books, tickets for a concert, dinner reservations, jewellery, silver goblets – the list is endless. I have even heard about a treasure chest being referred to as 'a fight box' – to be opened the first time the couple have a row, to remind them of how they felt on their wedding day.

Log sawing

When Anika and Dennis were married, they incorporated a tradition from Anika's grandmother. They had a log set up at the front of the ceremony room, and a large two-handled saw. The first task the couple faced once they were married was to saw the log in half, showing how by working together they could overcome any obstacle that was in their path. Dennis and Anika also used the log cutting in very practical terms, to depict turning an obstacle into firewood which would warm their home. Anika's father spoke some words about the need to keep the saw sharpened at all times, reflecting the ideal that Dennis and Anika should not be complacent but should work to keep the 'tools' of honesty, openness, and willingness to compromise alive and sharpened throughout the marriage.

Appendix 1 at the end of this book includes examples of some of the words which could be used in a simple quaich ceremony, treasure box ceremony, and taste ceremony.

Section 4: GESTURES OF LOVE AND PROTECTION

(see appendix 1 for sample wording)

At its heart, a marriage is about love. And we all have our own way of expressing and appreciating love. In his book, *The Five Love Languages,* Gary Chapman outlines five ways in which people feel loved: words of affirmation, acts of service, physical touch, receiving gifts, and spending quality time together. If you know what your preferences are, you could incorporate these into your wedding ceremony – offering a gift; making a simple physical gesture, e.g. washing feet or hands; giving your partner a watch, clock or diary, along with a commitment to spend time together; commissioning a poem or song; preparing and offering food or drink; or giving a duster and polish!

Eric and Beverly planted a tree in their garden. They promised to nurture and water the tree, and also to nurture their love. They anticipated watching the tree grow from year to year, its roots becoming firmer within the ground, and they anticipated watching their love grow and deepen over the forthcoming years. They trusted that the tree would help provide shelter and protection, and they trusted that they would shelter and protect each other from the storms of life.

A **rose ceremony** is another popular addition to a wedding. A red rose is an ancient symbol of love, and for a newly-married husband and wife to exchange a single red rose is a clear and simple way of expressing their love. A rose may be beautiful and fragrant yet it also comes with sharp thorns. In every marriage there are times when it is difficult, and each of you may be hurting. A rose symbolises that, despite the thorns, the love remains beautiful. Some couples use different coloured roses to depict different meanings and attributes:

Red rose – love and romance. 'I love you'

Pink rose – grace and elegance, a sign of gratitude and appreciation

White rose – symbolic of new beginnings, especially weddings, and of remembrance: 'I'm thinking of you'

Orange rose – full of energy, passion, and enthusiasm

Yellow rose – for joy, friendship, and warmth

A **truce bell** is another way of recognising the reality of married life and the inevitable moments of disagreement or conflict. Andy and Helen stood facing each other, filled with all the happiness of their wedding day and full of love and appreciation of each other. As they let the emotions flow through them, they each in turn picked up a bell and rang it. They made a commitment to remember the sound of the bell if they were having an argument or disagreement. And if resolution or compromise seemed difficult to reach, to ring the bell and signal a truce until some kind of resolution seemed more possible. Ringing the truce bell would remind them of their vows, and encourage them to resolve their differences compassion-ately and lovingly.

The fantasy series *Game of Thrones* includes **a cloaking ceremony** as part of a marriage. Although dramatised for the show, this ritual has its roots and origins in many different cultures and countries and was at one time the equivalent of exchanging rings. Typically, the bride and groom approached the altar wearing cloaks elaborately embroidered with the colours and crests of their respective family. After the vows, the bride's father would remove her cloak, symbolising that she was no longer in need of his protection. The husband would then welcome his bride into his family, and accept his role as her protector by draping her shoulders in a new cloak reflecting the colours and crests of his family.

Variations of this in other cultures offer a more equal approach where the bride and groom swap cloaks, or where they only put on cloaks (of a similar style) after their vows. In some Native American cultures, the couple each arrive wrapped in a blue blanket or shawl. After their vows, and to share their first kiss, they are wrapped together in a decorated white blanket or shawl, which then becomes a family heirloom, symbolic of mutual protection, shelter, warmth, adornment, rightful pride, sanctuary, privacy, and closeness. In other cultures and traditions, wrapping a shawl around the couple depicts that their love and marriage is wrapped in the wings of God.

Appendix 1 at the end of this book includes examples of some of the words which could be used in a tree planting or rose ceremony.

Section 5: INDIVIDUAL EXPRESSION and FAMILY TRADITIONS

Some couples come to their wedding with particular family traditions that they would like to include in the ceremony. In Chapter 9 there are some examples of these in Robbie and Christine's wedding, where Robbie gave Christine the silver sixpence given by his father to his mother many years before. Or the ceremony of Jesse and Laura, where Jesse wore odd shoes in remembrance of Laura's grandparents' wedding (you can read more about this in Chapter 9).

Other couples want something that is important in their lives together, something emblematic of their relationship or their approach to life. This may be as simple as decorating the ceremony room with important artefacts, or it may be more elaborate.

Chrissy had studied renaissance art. She and Gavin had been inspired by Botticelli's painting of Venus standing on a scallop shell, and also by the legend of Aphrodite, the Greek goddess of love and beauty being given a shell by Poseidon, the God of the Sea, to represent their love. Gavin and Chrissy planned to move to live by the beach, so they included lots of sea and beach-themed elements in their wedding. The bride's arrival was heralded by blowing a large conch shell – a Hawaiian tradition – and, instead of exchanging rings, Gavin and Chrissy exchanged a variety of shells, each with a different meaning: a scallop for truth and faithfulness; coral for warmth and openness; sea-urchin for boldness and confidence; a mussel for honesty and creativity; and a cowrie for prosperity and generosity.

Sharon and Izzy had a very tight budget for their wedding, but they still wanted something dramatic and wonderful so they decided to hold a masked ball. All their guests were invited to buy or create a mask to wear, and Izzy and Sharon arrived into the ceremony each wearing beautiful, ornately decorated masks in the style of a Venetian masquerade. They spoke about the importance of honesty and openness in their relationship, and at the point of making their vows they each took off their masks so they were open, honest and vulnerable with each other – it was a spectacular moment!

Gordon and Cara loved butterflies, and they liked the idea of including the symbolism of transformation and delicacy in their wedding ceremony. They had read about a couple who had released butterflies, but they considered it to be unkind and not entirely ethical to capture butterflies. So they used butterfly motifs in their decorations and on their stationery, and during their ceremony Gordon presented Cara with a beautiful butterfly brooch.

Section 6: GESTURES FROM TRADITION, CULTURE and RELIGION

(see appendix 1 for sample wording)

I preface this section with advice about being respectful to whichever tradition or culture a ritual or gesture is based in. For example, the tradition of a married couple jumping over a broom is often part of a pagan or Celtic ceremony, and yet it also has strong affiliation with the African-American community and it is good to understand the context of what you are doing rather than risk causing hurt or offence.

If you intend to include a symbolic gesture, such as the Jewish tradition of breaking a glass, or the Greek Orthodox tradition of exchanging a crown of flowers, please take advice from within your own family. Many traditions have multiple meanings and symbolisms, and it is important that you and your celebrant are clear on what you are trying to depict and that this is explained to your wedding guests.

In Jewish and other traditions, the groom **breaks a glass** at the end of the ceremony. These are the words that Shane and Eleanor chose for their wedding: '*Shane and Eleanor would like to conclude their ceremony with the traditional custom of breaking a glass. There are many things that glass can symbolise: the fragility of human relationships and the care that must be taken to nurture and look after these precious relationships; or fruitfulness – that happiness, and children, will be as numerous as the shards of glass. But for you, Shane and Eleanor, this is a reminder that the breaking of the glass, like the commitment you make today, is irrevocable and permanent.*'

In Sarah and Daniel's nature-based ceremony, they wanted to honour the four elements of life: '*As we pledge our hearts and our lives together, we honour the Earth for providing shelter and nourishment, Water for the flow of life itself, Fire for warmth and passion, and Air for every breath.*'

In Greek Orthodox traditions, the bride and groom are regarded as part of the royal family of God, and are crowned king and queen of their own dominion, their new fellowship, and family. The **wedding crowns**, called stephana, symbolise the glory and honour that is bestowed upon them by God, and the ribbon between the two stephana symbolises the unity of the couple. In

Vasileios and Colette's wedding, the best man blessed the crowns, placed them on the heads of Colette and Vasileios, and exchanged them three times. This was followed by the ceremonial walk around the altar with the bride and groom taking their first steps together into their married life – three times around the altar table, recognising the Holy Trinity and their happiness at the union of their two families.

Ben and Kelly included a Celtic variation of **jumping the broom**. At the end of their ceremony, Kelly and Ben stood facing down the aisle, and a broom decorated with fragrant herbs (rosemary, lavender, and willow for gratitude, grace, and adaptability) was held low down in front of them. The ends of the broom were held by Kelly's Dad and Ben's uncle, showing how the families provide the couple with the security of unconditional love and a source of tradition, heritage, and history. As Kelly and Ben stood in front of the broom, they honoured ancestors through the ages, previous generations, and all those who have been before them and have paved their way in life. The broom symbolised that the couple had swept away the old, and that problems and concerns were pushed aside. The couple were looking ahead to the future and were ready to step into their new life. As Ben and Kelly jumped the broom, they leapt forward into a joint future.

Ajit and Safa wore **flower garlands** during their wedding, representing happiness, enthusiasm, excitement, zeal, and beauty. As the strong thread runs through the delicate flower petal, so the strength of Safa and Ajit's marriage vows would run through their lives. The garlands were placed on their heads by their parents, symbolising acceptance and welcoming into the new family.

When Kim and Dominic were married, Kim's parents came from China to celebrate the wedding. Kim and Dominic included a **tea ceremony** as part of their marriage, to honour and show respect to the families. The bride and groom lit two wedding candles (one with a phoenix, the other with a dragon motif) to represent each of their families, and the table was decorated with white flowers, fruit, and burning incense, and of course a tea-set with the finest green tea.

Appendix 1 at the end of this book includes examples of some of the words which could be used in a Mexican Lazo ceremony, Greek crowning, or jumping the broom.

WHEN TO INCLUDE A SYMBOLIC GESTURE

It is important to think through the flow to your ceremony and to identify the point at which a symbolic gesture or ritual might be best placed. A ring warming usually comes early in the ceremony so that there is no delay in waiting for the rings to be returned. But when I've included a ring warming in very small weddings, those with only 10 or so guests, then I would suggest that blessing the rings is significant in itself and that the ring warming is completed immediately before the ring exchange.

Unity gestures, such as candle lighting, or gestures of love and protection such as exchanging a rose, are often completed right before the vows – it is a good point at which to focus attention, and to symbolise a couple's unity and commitment to the promises they are about to make.

I think that handfasting is particularly effective if the couple's hands are tied while they are saying their vows, but I have also performed handfastings at the end of the ceremony. In one wedding, the couple did not remove their hands from the ribbons, but instead they left the ceremony hand-in-hand together – still tied. Some folk-lore suggests that the hands should remain tied until after the marriage has been consummated, but I'm pretty certain that no-one adheres to that now!

Sharing a drink, breaking a glass, and jumping the broom are all rituals which sit well at the conclusion of the ceremony as the couple are about to leave. They add some theatre, as well as being a key moment for offering good wishes and blessing for the couple and their future life together.

Whatever you choose, this is your opportunity to create your own little moment in history – so be creative and have fun!

Chapter 9. Involving Other People in your Ceremony

Although marriage is essentially about two people coming together to make their vows and promises to one another, a marriage does not exist in isolation; it flourishes and is encouraged by all the friends and family who support it. It is always a special delight to have those you love participating in your ceremony in some way, and there are many approaches to this – some about individual contributions; some to reflect relationships of particular importance (such as including children in a marriage ceremony); and some which enable all your guests to be involved and to demonstrate their love and support.

I think it is lovely to acknowledge the importance of your family and friends from the start. Of course, in your speeches you may thank people and make special mentions, but it is always nice if the introductory words in the ceremony set the scene and appreciate that your guests have made an effort to be there, and that many have provided support and encouragement before this day. Chapter 2 includes some suggestions for how to include this in the welcome and opening words. However, beyond that, it can be touching and meaningful for others to play a significant role in your ceremony.

Involving individual friends or family members

People often find it a great honour, and something very moving, to be singled out and asked to participate in a couple's wedding ceremony, and correspondingly some may feel a bit disappointed if they think they have been left out or that others have been given a more prominent role. So the key consideration in involving others is tact and diplomacy! This may be particularly so if you have a complicated mix of parents and step-parents, or siblings who do not have a role as a bridesmaid or best man, or close friends who are not part of the main wedding party.

Chapter 7 offers some ideas about including readings in your ceremony, and this is a lovely way for others to be involved and to take a key role. As I suggested in that chapter, you should take care in choosing the people who read so that they feel confident and not overwhelmed by the task, and that you are clear about whether you are giving them something specific to read, whether they have the freedom to choose their own reading, or whether you are hoping and expecting that they will create something special and unique for you.

At Bobby and Regina's wedding, the bride's sister, Teresa, had recently had a baby and was unable to make the transatlantic flight to be at the ceremony. However, Teresa had recorded a song that she and Regina used to sing as teenagers. Regina was clearly moved by the addition to her wedding, and appreciated the effort that Teresa had made, as did her wedding guests – there was not a dry eye in the room!

Involving other people can also be a way to incorporate traditions or elements which are part of your culture or upbringing, but not central to your ceremony. In some of the weddings I have held, the couple are not religious and do not want a religious wedding, but it has been important for a key member of the family to offer a prayer or some words of blessing for the occasion and for the couple. When Aileen and Stewart were married, Aileen's grandfather brought an old family Bible to the wedding. He wanted to pass it on to Stewart and Aileen, and asked that they would sign the inside front page during the ceremony, adding their names to several previous generations. It was a lovely way to honour the traditions of the family over generations.

Often when couples tell me about the importance of their marriage, they talk about the examples shown by their parents, grandparents, or other relatives, and how they model the good parts of these marriages in their own relationship. If your parents or grandparents have long-lasting and happy marriages, it can be nice to acknowledge that, and to pick out a couple of particular attributes to mention: *'Peter and Shannon appreciate that they each grew up in loving and supportive families, and they learnt from a young age about some of the compromises which are necessary to retain a close and enduring marriage. Peter says that he hopes to emulate his parents' mutual respect, irrespective of their work or family roles, and their sense of mischievousness – no matter how old they were! And Shannon appreciates that her mum's determination and her dad's patience were important in keeping the family going when times were difficult.'*

As an alternative, family support and connection might be demonstrated through a symbolic gesture, for example having the fathers bring forward the family 'clan' tartan to be used in a Celtic handfasting (see chapter 8).

Elaine and Sandy included in their ceremony a ritual of sharing a drink from a Scottish quaich. Elaine's grandfather had made the quaich for them – lovingly carved out of pear wood from the trees in his garden – while Sandy's grandmother presented the couple with a rare bottle of malt whisky from the island which had been her childhood home. Then Elaine and Sandy's parents all joined the couple and sipped whisky from the quaich, demonstrating their support for the couple's marriage, and the creation of a new extended family.

Sometimes the important lessons in life and love come from those who are no longer alive, or there may be a desire to pass on some kind of heritage, for example, rings from parents or grandparents, or family jewellery remodelled into a wedding keepsake. When Don and Cara were married, Cara's Indian heritage was represented by a family necklace which her mother fastened around her neck during the ceremony.

Often ancestors or family members are acknowledged through the lighting of a candle – maybe using the 'ancestral flame' as the source point for lighting the other candles in a unity candle ceremony.

There are many ways of acknowledging family and their traditions. These are a few of my favourites:

Both Sven and Katya came from families with complicated sets of relationships, and neither of them had the surname of their biological parents. They decided that after their marriage they would revert to ancestral family names to honour their bloodline, and they created a new family surname for themselves which incorporated the names of their grandparents.

When Jesse and Laura were married, Jesse appeared at the wedding in an extremely smart suit. However, looking down, it could be seen that Jesse was wearing one very smart, highly polished black shoe, and one rather scruffy, down-at-heel brown shoe. We explained this during the ceremony: 'Some of you may have noticed Jesse is wearing two different shoes—and no, that's not because he is a bad dresser—but, instead, it is to honour the love and admiration Laura has for her late grandfather. On Laura's grandparents' wedding day, her grandfather got married wearing two different shoes, because he simply could not afford a matching pair. This shows that true love doesn't require pomp and circumstance; true love is deeper than appearance, and with these different shoes Jesse hopes his marriage to Laura is as strong and as loving as Laura's grandparents' was.' The wearing of odd shoes was a surprise for Laura, and added great warmth and lots of laughter to the ceremony.

When Robbie and Christine were married, all their family from Ireland had travelled to join them in their celebration. When Robbie's father got married, he had presented his wife with a silver sixpence to symbolise that all his possessions and riches were to be shared with his wife. The same sixpence had been gifted to Robbie, and he presented it to Christine *during the ceremony to show the same commitment as his father had: Robbie (addressing Christine): 'This gift of a silver coin is a symbol of my firm intention to share with you all of my worldly goods, to offer my possessions to you gladly and willingly, believing that whatever was mine, is now yours, too.'*

Creating a Family Feel

If those who are close to you are not going to be the best speakers or readers, or if they decline the offer, there are several other ways in which you can include them. Performers may be willing to play music or sing, talented sewers or craft-lovers may help with making clothes/outfits/decorations. Some people may have a particular talent – making a cake, or being the photographer. Some people may prefer to have a role behind the scenes – decorating the venue, looking after official paperwork, or helping guests to their seats. Other family or friends may have specific roles during your ceremony – e.g. bringing the rings, being an official witness and signing the register, bringing items for a symbolic gesture.

When Jen and Mo were married, Mo's aunts from Algeria brought a richly decorated shawl as a wedding gift, and during the ceremony they wrapped it around the shoulders of Mo and Jen with these words: 'The relationship between a husband and wife is like a garment, a cloak or a shawl that you wrap around each other. As you are wrapped together in this shawl, may you be similarly wrapped together in love – and may both shawl and love, each in their own way, offer you protection and adornment, comfort, shelter, and support.

Steph and Ken wanted to show how important their grandmothers had been in their lives, but everything they thought of seemed too serious or emotional, and didn't capture the sense of fun and joy which they wanted to depict. Neither Ken nor Steph had any young children in their families, so they lit upon the idea of asking their grandmothers to be flower-girls, or flower-nans as they re-named them. At the start of the wedding, I announced the arrival of the bridal party. And first to enter were four charming ladies, aged from 72-84, giggling like little girls, smiling and waving at the guests, and strewing petals from flower baskets. They were having great fun, and it really set the tone for a delightful, happy family occasion.

Reflecting Important Relationships

It is not unusual for couples getting married to already have children – either children that one or both parties have from previous relationships, who will become part of a new and different family group, or children that the couple have had between them before getting married. It is nice to give special acknowledgement to children from the start of the ceremony, and to be clear about the dual nature of the event – a marriage of two people AND a celebration of family. The wedding may be the point at which all family members live in one home, or it may be the point at which everyone takes on the same name. Even if there are no obvious outward signs or demonstrable changes to how the family members live day-to-day, the marriage formalises the relationship that the couple have with each other and with their children – husband, wife, step-parents, step-brothers and step-sisters – and all kinds of other blended opportunities.

Sometimes it is enough to mention the children and to acknowledge their presence and their importance, but it can be lovely to actively include them in the ceremony too. Blended families can be beautifully depicted and celebrated with a unity candle or family candle, or with a sand ceremony to show the important place a child has within the family, and to demonstrate the protection that the love of the parents offers them.

When Donna and Liam were married, they wanted to include all four children in their handfasting. In addition to the ribbons for Liam and Donna, each child brought forward another ribbon and tied it into the other, so that when the handfasting knot was completed it tied all the family members together as one.

Ian and Carlotta also wanted to include their children in their handfasting, but they were too young to play any active role. So Carlotta created a beautiful plaited handfasting cord made from three strands of material – one for her, one for Ian, and one for their children. She sewed onto it tiny charms for each of the children, and also charms for their parents.

Unfortunately, not all families join together amicably, and for various reasons it may be that children, or other important people, are not present, or are present but clearly want no visible role. In situations like this, it is always helpful to talk to your celebrant, who will be able to help you decide how they can be incorporated with love and tact and care.

Other lovely ways to include children in a wedding ceremony can be the presentation of special gifts. Anna and Royston gave their children special necklaces, each with a silver jigsaw piece. Together the jigsaw pieces matched up to create one whole, representative of how each person was a vital piece of the whole family jigsaw.

For Kitty and Arnie, their marriage was a commitment to each other and also a commitment to create a stable home and family for their children. Arnie and Kitty made their vows to each other, and then they turned to the children and made vows to them. These were Arnie's vows: 'When I chose to marry Kitty, I also chose to create a new family, one that includes us all. If any of you feel sad, then I feel sad, too; if you are happy, then I am happy, too.

Lucien, you inspire me, I am proud to be your dad and I thank you for accepting Kitty into our world. I promise to cherish and guide you, and to support you always.

Emily, I wasn't there when you took your first steps, but I promise you now that I will love and support you in every step that you take in the future.

To you both, I promise to listen to you, show you respect, kindness, and tolerance, and encourage you as an individual. I acknowledge the past and all that has led to the creation of our new family, and I accept the responsibilities of parenthood – shared with others. I will strive to bring love and security for our life together.'

In other ceremonies involving children, the vows may be much simpler. Kirsten and Marty had two young sons at the time of their marriage. They thought that they might have more children in their future, so wanted any words to be inclusive of any additional children in the family. They added a simple line to their vows: *'I will be a loving and equal partner to you, and a loving and equal parent to our children.'*

Occasionally, I have been asked to create ceremonies in which the children also make vows. If you plan to do this, it is important that you know whether your children really want to participate in this way, and to have a well thought-through contingency plan in case one (or more) child does not want to speak at the last minute. You don't want to have a situation where three out of four children make a family vow, and one child ends up feeling left out. Nor do you want a child feeling under pressure to be involved. If you do decide to include this, it is a good idea if each child is involved in writing or contributing to the words they will say, and I always suggest that it should be simple, and preferably something which is possible for the child to follow through on. For example: 'Today I am happy to be part of this family.' I think it is particularly tough to have any expectation that children will promise to love or respect a parent, step-parent or sibling, or to make a commitment to honour the family. Even if an enthusiastic and sincere child or young adult makes the suggestion of including a promise, it really is something to be approached with great thought and care.

Dual Ceremonies

Sometimes, and particularly if a child is very young, a couple will want to include a naming ceremony as part of the event, and to take the opportunity to do this while closest family and friends are already gathered together.

Although united by a common family bond, each ceremony has a very distinct feeling and purpose, so it is important to think about how the two will be conducted and how the timing of each relates to the other. The following is an extract and description from Lesley and Lee's wedding ceremony and baby Katie's naming ceremony:

'This is a wonderful family occasion celebrating the bonds that span generations, with lots of children sharing in the excitement, and appreciation for grandparents who have been important in your lives. We also welcome the arrival of little Katie into this family, and make promises and commitments to love and support her.'

The celebration started with Lee and Lesley's marriage ceremony, during which they lit a unity candle. As part of the subsequent naming ceremony, Katie's godparents lit a candle for her as they made their promises to love and support her and offer her advice and friendship. Lesley and Lee made their own promises to love and teach Katie, to create for her a safe, kind, and loving home, and to nurture her with patience and tolerance. They then used the flame from their marriage unity candle, along with the flame from Katie's candle, to light a family candle.

Then all the family and friends took the opportunity to welcome Katie as part of their family and community, and also to give Lee and Lesley their love, support, and encouragement in raising their child. Guests lit their own small candles as they made the commitment to surround the whole family with their care, that day and in the years to come.

Heather and Bobby took an alternative approach. They had invited close friends and family to the christening/welcoming ceremony for their children, Tamara and Joel. It was a wonderful day, with the ceremony held in their garden under the fruit trees, and Heather wearing a light, white summer dress. The garden was decorated with bunting and hearts, and it all seemed like a very appropriate setting for the welcoming ceremony. At the conclusion, Bobby and Heather stepped forward and faced their guests. I reminded everyone of the vows that they had made to provide stability and security for the children, and then announced that Bobby and Heather had concluded that the best way to provide that, and to demonstrate their commitment to the family, was by getting married. We then proceeded to have a short but meaningful wedding ceremony – a wonderful surprise for all the guests (although obviously planned meticulously by the couple, their two legal witnesses, and myself).

Children at Weddings

Obviously there are times when children will be in attendance at a wedding ceremony, but I know that the question of whether to invite the children of family members and other guests is a topic which causes a lot of debate. However light-hearted and family-orientated the whole occasion is intended to be, there are moments during a marriage ceremony when it is undoubtedly a formal and significant event. This can be quite boring for children, especially if they've waited in the ceremony room for upwards of 15 minutes before proceedings begin, or if they've already been on their best behaviour for several hours while getting ready.

If the couple – or many of their close family and friends – have children, it may not be practical not to have young children present, and it may be your opinion that a wedding is a family event and that all are welcome. Whether it is your own children, or those of your guests, be clear about what your ideas and expectations are. Maybe all and everything is welcome; perhaps you are happy for children to wander around quietly, but to be encouraged to leave if they are getting upset; or maybe you want to make sure that there is an adjacent room with toys – and the wedding ceremony on a video link – so that parents can feel relaxed about taking children out of the ceremony, and don't have to worry about missing the whole event themselves.

There is a big difference between a baby making a few gurgles, an eight-year-old asking poignant questions, a happily chattering four-year-old, and a hot, over-tired child who is becoming distressed at a parent trying to keep them away from candles or heavy flower arrangements. At Scott and Debbie's wedding, their two daughters were beautiful and cute bridesmaids. They were soon joined at the front of the church by their two cousins, and then by their cousins' older brother, who started a chase around – and under – the table.

When Sean and Julie lit a candle during their wedding ceremony, it was a poignant moment intended to honour and acknowledge grandparents and other family members who had passed on. Their three-year-old son promptly blew the candle out and sang a lovely rendition of Happy Birthday ☺

These are amusing anecdotes, and such occurrences often break the tension, put nerves at bay, and help people to laugh and relax. But for others, they can be an unwelcome intrusion into a very special and significant occasion.

Involving Pets

This may seem frivolous and a bit quirky, but often for a couple getting married a central aspect of their day-to-day life is loving and taking responsibility for pets, and I frequently have requests for ways in which pets can be included and involved in a ceremony. Of course, you may be constrained by your venue, which may not permit animals, but I have to be guided by the couple in this, and I always urge caution. Most often, the pet is a dog, and the dog may have a specific role. In Eddie and Joey's wedding, their little dog, Meatball, was one of the bridal party and she arrived with the bridesmaids, all dressed up in a matching yellow satin dog outfit. Sometimes a dog will bring the rings into the ceremony – look online, and there are lots of ways to affix a ring cushion to a dog's collar. This can work well if your pet is a stable, placid, unflustered animal, but often a pet will sense the excitement and react either by becoming frightened and withdrawing under a chair, or over-excited and wanting to jump up and be involved – usually not what a bride wants when she is wearing a delicate white lace dress. So sometimes it is simpler, and kinder, to bring your pet for the photos, or include them in another way, such as a poem or a funny story.

Involving All Your Guests

A wedding is about more than close family and friends – it is the joining of families, and the extension of a community of family and friends. If most of your guests have been accustomed to attending church weddings and you have chosen to have a non-religious ceremony with no hymns or collective prayers, then some of them may feel a little uninvolved in your ceremony – observers, rather than active supporters.

It can feel more inclusive if your family and friends can demonstrate their support by participating in a ring warming, tying ribbons or messages to a wishing tree, placing wish pebbles in a bowl, adding sand following a unity sand ceremony, building a cairn of stones, or helping to create a special memento for the couple.

Bill and Ali are both keen amateur chefs, who love to travel and to learn new recipes from around the world. Guests to their wedding were invited to bring herbs and spices – each with a significant meaning for the couple and their marriage. There was an amazing array of wit and creativity: almonds for hope; some olive oil to help communication to run smoothly; chilies and curry powder for warmth and a little spice; dried fruit for when more energy is needed in the relationship; and an apple wrapped in a padlock, to keep them free of temptation! Guests placed these in a basket before the ceremony, giving me time to select a few to incorporate into a blessing of good wishes during Ali and Bill's ceremony.

Many of the suggestions above are included during the reception, but it is lovely if you can draw the link to the ceremony if the process is started there. For example, the parents and bridal party making their marks on a thumb print tree as an integral part of the ceremony, and other guests adding to it as they leave the ceremony or during a drinks reception. Or following the example of Corrinne and Don, who included a tree planting ceremony in their outdoor wedding, and then gave all their guests a tiny tree sapling as wedding favours. For Don and Corrinne, the tree symbolised their hope for growth, new life, strong roots, and adaptability.

Douglas and Mhairi had a very Scottish wedding – bagpipes, fiddle music, and lots of traditional customs. During the wedding ceremony, Douglas took a piece of tartan which was fashioned into a brooch. He turned to his guests and explained: 'The life I have with Mhairi is like a piece of tartan – we each bring our different characteristics or colours to the relationship. I bring a strong green – it represents my love of the outdoors and nature, and my strong belief in conservation and peace. Mhairi brings a beautiful red – cheerful, and warm, and striking. These colours can be seen clearly in the tartan; a block of green and a block of crimson. And yet, I can see where these threads overlap and combine, and they form a beautiful autumnal brown. I also bring some threads of blue, my hesitation and fear of trying anything new! And yes, also my stability and reliability. Mhairi brings some threads of brown – her stubbornness, but also her determination never to give up. There are threads of yellow for the sunshine in our lives, and a few threads of black and grey. If we peer closely, we can see all the different threads and where they have come from. However, the real joy and beauty of our life together is when we stand back and look at the whole fabric, and see the richness of the tartan.

We are two individuals, but our lives are woven together and that new pattern is what makes our relationship and our marriage unique.' Douglas then pinned the tartan brooch onto Mhairi's dress, and he invited all his guests to take a similar tartan bow and to pin it to a wife, or husband, or partner, or family member, or friend, to acknowledge and celebrate the richness and beauty of their own relationships.

Rather than a physical gesture, it can be wonderful to involve your guests in saying something collectively, for example, your family and friends together saying some words of blessing during the lighting of a unity candle.

This is the blessing that guests recited at Stuart and Natalie's wedding: 'As the new flame burns undivided, so your lives will be one, blessed and strengthened in your love. Like the bright flame of the candle, may there always be evidence of your love, may it lighten any dark times, and may everyone around you feel its warmth.'

In other ceremonies, guests join together in expressing their love and support for the couple in a 'charge to the guests'. This can be early in the ceremony, with family and friends showing their support for the marriage ceremony; it could be immediately before the vows, allowing guests to show their commitment to support the couple in upholding the promises they make to each other; or it could be at the end of the ceremony, with friends and family bestowing their good wishes for the newly-married couple's future. Chapter 10 offers some examples of words which can be used for this.

Whether your wedding has hundreds of guests or just a few, each of them is there because they bring something special to the lives of the couple getting married. It is these family and friends who will support and encourage your marriage over the years to come, and it is wonderful to think of ways in which their commitment and love can be shown during your ceremony.

Chapter 10: Creating a Stunning Finish

I f you've followed the book so far, you'll have seen how we create a warm welcome for you and your guests, included something of your personal journey and the vision for your future, and perhaps included some readings or symbolic gestures. You've said your vows and made lasting promises, and now THIS is the moment that everyone has been waiting for – the high point of your ceremony when your celebrant or officiant makes the pronouncement:

'You are now husband and wife.'

Often the couple embrace, the guests clap and cheer, and the photographer is standing by to capture the perfect snap of the first married kiss!

Depending on where in the world your marriage is taking place, and whether your ceremony is religious or not, there may be a set form of words for the pronouncement of marriage. The statement may be very simple: 'Dave and Rita, you are now married.' Or it may prolong the anticipation of the guests by recapping – very briefly – on the process and mood of the ceremony, including some of the following phrases:

Name of the couple:

Rita and Dave

Legal or other authority

Here in the state of California/by the authority of the
Registrar General of Scotland/in the name of a loving
God

Context of the ceremony

In the presence of God/here in nature beneath a
lovely blue sky/with your family and friends as your
witnesses/surrounded by those closest to you...

Process of the ceremony

You have made your promises to one another/
you have shown your commitment by exchanging
rings/you have bound your hands in a handfasting/
promised to unite your family as one/committed for
eternity...

Statement of marriage

I pronounce you are now husband and wife/partners
in marriage/a married couple.

The Kiss

In Western weddings, it is customary for couples to
share a kiss at this point. In days gone by, the bride may
have worn a veil over her face until this moment, when
the veil would then be lifted and a chaste kiss would

be planted on her cheek. These days, there is rarely a veil and there is often considerably more exuberance to celebrate this momentous occasion. ☺

The most traditional words at this point are 'you may now kiss your bride', however some couples feel uncomfortable that their celebrant is giving permission for the husband to kiss his wife, and alternative words include: 'you may now share your first kiss as a married couple', or encouragement to seal their marriage with a kiss, or celebrate with a kiss, or simply left to the couple to do whatever happens spontaneously.

When Brendan and Rebecca were married, they were uncomfortable with the planned or rehearsed nature of the wedding kiss and planned to celebrate with a high five, but in the event it was followed by a spontaneous hug and kiss, anyway.

If you do plan to kiss, your photographer may well encourage you to make sure that the moment lasts long enough so that he/she can catch a photo of the special moment, and the delighted look on your faces afterwards. Although, the kiss shouldn't last so long that your guests are getting embarrassed!

Practicalities

Depending on the location of your wedding and the legal process, the pronouncement may be followed immediately by the signing of official documents (signing the register in the UK). In Scotland, this is often done in full view in the ceremony room, or it may be completed off to the side in an adjacent room. Either way, this is an excellent point in which to have a musical interlude, which helps to keep the process as an integral part of the ceremony and doesn't break the mood.

Once the formalities are completed, the couple take their place before their guests, facing them for the first time as a married couple. It may be enough for the couple to leave at this point, accompanied by the chosen recessional music, but it can be nice to complete the ceremony by adding in some closing elements. This might be a symbolic ritual, such as a unity sand ceremony, breaking a glass, or sharing a drink from a loving cup (see chapter 8 for details and examples).

At the conclusion of Farhana and Ewen's marriage, they had prepared a drink of Sharbat (a sweet fruity drink) for all their guests, so that they could share in their joy and drink to their health.

Celebrant: The years of your life together are like a cup of Sharbat poured out for you to drink. Sharbat is sweet – symbolic of happiness, joy, hope, peace, love, and delight. As you all share the drink, you undertake to share all that the future may bring. All the sweetness that life may hold for each of you will be even sweeter because you drink it together. And as all family and friends who have come to witness and celebrate this marriage drink their Sharbat, we celebrate your marriage, we commit to supporting you, and we wish you a sweet marriage, happiness, and health.

As in the example above, the close of the ceremony is also a point at which the bride and groom might thank their guests, and an opportunity for guests to show their support for the couple and their marriage.

Bride and Groom thank their guests

During the ceremony, the bride and groom are often facing each other. The end of the ceremony provides an opportunity to turn and face friends and family, while the officiant thanks everyone for all their support. This is a beautiful way to treasure the moment of seeing everyone who is there for you on your special day.

These are the words I used during Will and Celia's wedding:

'Celia and Will, you stand now before those that you love and those who love you. Here are the family and friends who raised you, taught you, supported you, and shaped your lives. Will and Celia appreciate the example of marriage shown to them by their parents, Charles and Davina, and Carol and Stan – you have taught them the importance and the value of love. Celia and Will thank you, and thank all of you for the profound and positive influence you have been in their lives. So now, Celia and Will, say simply: Thank you.'

Affirmation of the Community

A gesture such as the bride and groom's thank you, is often linked to the Affirmation of the Community – it is an opportunity for family and friends to participate, and to voice their support for the newly-married couple.

Here are some examples for you to consider:

Now that you have heard BRIDE and GROOM exchange their vows, do you, their family and friends, promise to encourage and support them in creating a strong and vital marriage?

If so, say, 'We do.'

OR

A new family has been created this afternoon, and we are here to welcome them and celebrate their new relationship. Do you – their family and friends – promise, from this day forward, to encourage them and love them, to give them your guidance, and to support them in being true to the promises that they have made?

If yes, say, 'We do.'

OR

The marriage of BRIDE and GROOM unites two families and creates a new community. Will you, who are gathered here today, bless and support their marriage?

If so, please answer, 'We will.'

OR

As friends and family of this newly-married couple, you occupy an important place in their lives, and they ask your blessings for their marriage. So BRIDE and GROOM ask you to reach out to them in times of trouble, and help them to celebrate their achievements and their joys.

Will you, who are present here today, surround BRIDE and GROOM in love and support them in their marriage?

If so, please answer, 'We will.'

Closing words and Blessing

The vows have been said, the rings exchanged, the couple have kissed, and the paperwork is signed. So how are we going to close the ceremony?

The Blessing of the Marriage is the conclusion to a wedding ceremony and comes just before the bride and groom are introduced as a couple, or pronounced as husband and wife. A blessing at the end of the marriage ceremony is like a seal of joy and good wishes for the future. It doesn't have to be religious, although it may be if you are having a religious ceremony, and the words of blessing can be read by your celebrant, or officiant, or by one of your guests. At a recent wedding, the bride's younger sister, aged 10, read from the Debbie Gliori book, *No Matter What*.

Blessings may be a traditional prayer or might be based on words from a book or poem, such as the traditional Apache Blessing, or the Celtic or Irish Blessing. There are many variations of these, so take time to find one that says the words which are right for you. This is one of my favourite versions of a Celtic Blessing:

May the road rise to meet you.

May the wind be always at your back.

May the sun shine warm upon your face,

And the rains fall soft upon the fields.

May the light of friendship guide your paths together.

May the laughter of children grace the halls of your home.

May the joy of living for one another bring a smile to your lips, a twinkle to your eye.

The whole length of your joy-filled days.

Here are some other ideas of closing blessings to inspire you:

Blessing for growth

Go into the world and fulfil your dreams.

Love, support, and help one another as you grow.

Seek out opportunities to be good to each other.

May the seeds of your love, now planted in marriage, continue to grow.

May your life together be an example of love spreading outward to your family, your friends, and to the wider circle of the world.

OR

Themes of day and night

Each day of your life together,

May the sun rise on new joys and new treasures for you to discover,

And each evening,

May it set peacefully on a world made bright and beautiful by the love you share.

OR

Reflection of personal ideals and values (peace, understanding, compassion, friendship being together, home)

From this day forward, may you live together in peace.

May you grow each day in understanding and compassion.

When you are apart, may you return to one another in togetherness.

May the home you establish be a place of sanctuary, where many will find a welcome.

OR

Themes of family

In your marriage, may you broaden your family circle, remember your heritage, and recall those who gave you life.

Call upon your ancestors, the foundations of your families, and always in your thoughts.

Call upon the elders in your community, whose wisdom you seek in all endeavours, your friends, who are a delight in your lives, and your parents, who have guided you along the road to adulthood.

Delight in the prospect of children, and create for them a peaceful, stable home of love, as a foundation on which they can build their lives.

OR

Blessing from nature

*We stand here amongst the trees in the presence of
Universal love, to affirm the commitment of this couple.
This is the day and the time of the new moon, a time for
new beginnings, for moving gently yet deliberately into
a new phase, for setting intention, and accepting the
wonder and mystery of life.*

*We honour the elements within and without, and call
on them to celebrate the coming together of [BRIDE]
and [GROOM].*

We thank the earth for providing shelter and nourishment
Water for the flow of life itself
Fire for warmth and passion
Air for every breath
Wood for the urge to act.

OR

The blessing of life's journey

*BRIDE and GROOM have come a long way. From
(insert reference to how the couple met), to declaring
their devotion to each other today. Theirs is a
continuing journey.*

*They may face challenges in life, the ups and downs of a
winding road,*

Now they begin their journey down the road of life together.

We don't know what lies ahead, for the road turns and bends.

Their task now is to find joy and exhilaration in change, and purpose in the new roads travelled.

No matter what direction is taken, these two people are explorers, embarking on a journey to wonderful new destinations.

Handfasting blessing (linked to the ritual or symbolic gesture of handfasting, which was part of the ceremony)

The ribbons that bound your hands, and the words that you have spoken, symbolise so much – your life, your love, and the eternal connection that the two of you have found with one another.

In the binding of the ribbons, may you remember the binding of your words.

So now there are two lives, but tied together in one heart, one home.

May these lives bound together, remain entwined forever.

May your hands be always clasped in friendship, and your hearts forever joined in love.

OR

Blessing following the sharing of a drink from a quaich or a loving cup

BRIDE and GROOM, as you have shared the drink from this cup, so may you share your lives. May you explore life's mysteries together and find life's joys heightened, its bitterness sweetened, and all of your life enriched by the love of family and friends. May you have happiness, and find it in making one another happy. May you have love, and find it in loving one another.

OR

Personal ideals and values (love, trust, willingness, faith, commitment)

To make your relationship work, will take love – this is the core of your marriage and why you are here today.

It will take trust, to know that in your hearts you truly want what is best for each other.

It will take willingness, to stay open to one another – and to learn and grow together.

It will take faith, to go forward together, without knowing exactly what the future brings.

And it will take commitment, to hold true to the journey you both have pledged to today.

OR

Celebration and blessings of Love

It was love that brought you here today.

It's love that makes yours a glorious union. And it will be love that makes your marriage endure.

Love will support you on your journey. Wherever life may carry you, you will stay by each other's side.

I therefore join with everyone gathered here today in extending to you our love and support, and our wish for your relationship to flourish and grow throughout a long and happy life together – always in love.

Simple blessing (1)

May you have love, and find it in loving one another; may you have happiness, and find it in making one another happy.

OR

Simple blessing (2)

In your marriage we wish you truth, understanding, fulfilment, peace…

OR

Simple blessing (3)

May love's blessing rest upon you, may love's peace abide with you, may love's presence live always in your hearts, now and for evermore.

OR

Simple blessing (4)

May the Spirit of love live always in your hearts.

May your relationship be a great and wonderful adventure.

May the mysteries of life be with you.

May your hope and security be in knowing that you are part of one another's life.

Simple blessing (5)

May love bless you and keep you close; may love shine in your lives, and be gracious to you; may love support you and encourage you, and give you peace.

If none of these options appeal to you, you could make your ceremony completely personal right to the end and create a blessing based on the things which are important for your future. This might include both those things that the two of you hope for yourselves, and also those things that your guests would wish for you.

As guests arrived at Samantha and Howie's wedding, they were encouraged to write a card and hang it on a blessings tree. I noted down the wishes that family and friends had made for Howie and Sam's future, and incorporated them into a blessing which I read at the close of the ceremony:

Sam and Howie, we are here to celebrate your marriage and also to offer you the gift of our blessings.

We wish for you love — a love that brings out the best in you, as you bring out the best in each other, that gives you something to lean on when you need it most.

Love that allows you to see each other as you really are, reminding you why you're together.

We wish for you a home — more than just a place to live, but a haven from the pressures of the world outside your door.

A home where you can let down your guard, unburden yourself, and know that there's someone always on your side.

Finally, we wish for you joy — a joy that makes you laugh out loud.

A joy that lights your eyes and fills your soul.

And a joy that shouts to the world of your happiness with one another.

All this and more we wish for you today, and every day throughout the years of your marriage.

Presentation of the Couple

The Presentation of the Couple is where the bride and groom are introduced as husband and wife for the first time. I always give guests encouragement to clap and cheer, and blow whistles, or whatever, as I invite guests to stand, and I say: 'Ladies and Gentlemen, it is my privilege to present to you for the very first time, Ann and Barry as...'

Before your wedding day, give some thought to how you want to be introduced. You might decide to take the same name, or not. Sometimes couples create a whole new name, a mix of their two existing names, or take an ancestral name. Sometimes if couples are uncertain about what names they will use, I might introduce them as husband and wife, or the newly-married couple.

'Ladies and Gentlemen, family and friends, it is my pleasure to present, for the first time anywhere, Stan and Julia as Mr. and Mrs. Bothwell.'

'And now, to all the friends and family who have come to celebrate this marriage, I would like to present, the newly-married couple Mr. and Mrs. Calder, and with their children Ben and Eve, as the Calder family.'

'Ladies and Gentleman, for those of you who have come to witness this union, it is my pleasure to present the newlyweds, Sandra and Dick.'

'And now, to all the friends and family who have come to celebrate this marriage, I take great pleasure in presenting Charlotte and Ian, husband and wife.'

A special event to end the ceremony

In some weddings, there is a special event to mark the conclusion of the ceremony. As with the inclusion of symbolic gestures and rituals, think about the meaning of what you are doing and the reason you are choosing that particular event to be included.

Releasing Doves

Doves have been used for centuries to symbolise the hope, peace, and love that come from new beginnings. As they are released into flight, they soar together in synchronous movement, creating beautiful patterns, and always in harmony with one another. Releasing doves represents unity, beauty, and peace, and symbolises two people moving together, each on their own path, yet united in their journey. As the birds are released into flight, the bride and groom send with them their own hopes and dreams, which will soar with the birds, and return to settle at a future point.

As always, be cautious and thoughtful about using animals or birds during your ceremony. In Suzie and

Elmer's wedding, they had a beautiful film clip of doves soaring, and they had feathers instead of confetti for the guests to throw.

Butterflies

Butterflies are beautiful and fragile. They symbolise the completion of a transformation process which echo the transformation that marriage brings.

If a butterfly lands on the palm of your hand, you cannot hold onto that butterfly. If you try to hold it, it will be crushed. But if you keep your hand open, it will be safe. This mirrors the respect and freedom of a marriage relationship – enticing one another yet not compelling them; enfolding each other in love without confining or crushing them. Just like our relationships, the butterfly needs to be free.

Bringing the symbolism of butterflies into your ceremony sounds wonderful and I have witnessed an incredibly moving moment when hundreds of butterflies took flight. However, it is important to be ethical and kind, and there are other fun ways to create a butterfly effect. You can buy paper butterflies on sticks, which flap their wings when you move the stick, or your guests can create a butterfly with their hands. To do this, hold your hands up in front of you with your palms facing you; move your right hand to the left, and your left hand to the right; interlock your thumbs; and flutter your fingers to create your own fragile butterfly.

Bubbles

Mitch and Sara-Jane had given their guests a bottle of bubbles, and as Sara-Jane and Mitch were leaving, I asked everyone to join in extending their love and support by taking a moment to believe in magic – how colour and light and a perfect circle come out of a breath and a stick – such simple ingredients. Guests focussed on their wishes for Mitch and Sara-Jane's relationship to flourish and grow throughout a long and happy life together. Then, taking a deep breath, they sent their wishes, blessings, and prayers out for the bride and groom as they sent their bubbles out into the sunshine.

As the recessional music plays, it is easy to make your wedding ceremony exit just as exciting as your entrance, with guests waving streamers, flags, bubbles, sparklers, kids' party-style tambourines, or kazoos. ☺

Walking out

The recessional is when the bride and groom walk back down the aisle to leave the ceremony, followed by the immediate members of the wedding party. The couple should brief the organist, musicians, or music co-ordinator, on what music they would like played during the recessional. There is generally an atmosphere of great happiness and relief; the vows have been made, the celebrations are about to begin, and the couple are officially married. The traditional order for the recessional is as follows: bride and groom, followed by chief bridesmaid and best man, followed by mother of the bride and father of the groom, followed by father of the bride and mother of the groom, and finally the other bridesmaids, baby bridesmaids and pages. It is nice to allow time for the bridal party to have private congratulations before all your guests follow you.

Logistics

As with the beginning of the ceremony, you need to get the logistics ironed out. Make sure you've arranged for helpers to organise the other guests. Specific requests about the exit can be announced by the celebrant, or by a master of ceremonies, e.g. 'please head to the front steps, grab a pack of confetti, a sparkler (or whatever), and line up on either side of the steps, so we can cheer the couple into their married life.' And then stick to your plans. Don't be thwarted by the sudden good idea that your photographer has just had.

Please be careful about the temptation to start hugging everyone on the way out. Or getting into an impromptu line-up leaving other guests waiting behind them. If you can, move well away from the exit to the room. Or, if you plan to have a receiving line, you would want to exit and wait just outside the door to greet guests as they make their way out.

But the most important thing...

RELAX, PARTY, CELEBRATE – you're married! ☺☺☺

In 1943, German theologian Dietrich Bonhoeffer wrote a letter to a young bride and groom, reminding them that 'it is not your love that sustains the marriage, but from now on, the marriage that sustains your love'

Appendix 1

Sample Extracts from Ceremonies

As you read parts of the book, particularly Chapter 8 about symbolic gestures and rituals, you may have come across something that interested you and you would like to know a little more. Perhaps the best way to illustrate these is by following the same structure as Chapter 8 and inserting some sample extracts from wedding ceremonies I have held, so this part of the book has examples of Unity Rituals, Gestures of Commitment, Gestures of Trust and Sharing, Gestures of Love and Protection, Individual Expression and Family Traditions, and Gestures from Tradition, Culture and Religion.

Of course there are many other ways in which to present these rituals, and your celebrant will help you to find words which suit your occasion and the sentiment which you want to express.

To avoid the anodyne use of 'groom' and 'bride' I have retained the couple's names – so these are actual ceremony extracts from real people's weddings. I hope they provide some explanation of different rituals and inspiration for your own ceremony.

Included here are some examples of words for:

- Unity candle ceremony

- Unity sand ceremony

- Cake ceremony

- Salt ceremony

- Fisherman's knot

- Three stranded knot

- Celtic (Scottish) handfasting

- Neo-pagan type handfasting

- Oathing stone

- Quaich ceremony (sharing a drink)

- Lock and Key

- Food Sharing

- Tree planting

- Rose ceremony

- Mexican Lazo

- Greek crowning

- Jumping the Broom

UNITY RITUALS

Unity Candle Ceremony

Celebrant: Today is the day when Michael and Siobhan step forward from being two people in love, into two people who are making a commitment of their lives and their love. As they step forward towards that life together, they symbolise their union by lighting a unity candle. Firstly, I invite them to light two individual candles – these represent Siobhan and Michael as individuals, and the flames of the candles reflect all the personality, qualities, and love that Michael and Siobhan each bring to their relationship and their marriage.

Michael and Siobhan step forward and each light a single candle.

Celebrant: Each candle has a flame that is bright and warm, it can stand on its own and be perfect and beautiful. Yet when these flames are used together to light a unity candle, they create a new light, a new brightness, and a new hope for life and love. You do not lose your individuality, and yet in marriage you are united as one. So, as Michael and Siobhan commit to their new life together, they symbolise their intention, joining in marriage and family as one, and using the flames of their individual candles together to light one unity candle. As you do so, we ask that that single flame, uniting both your lives, burns with the brightness of everything which joins you in marriage: creativity, caring, light-heartedness, and always seeing the positive.

Michael and Siobhan use the flames of their two individual candles to light the unity candle together.

Celebrant: As this new flame burns undivided, so your lives will be one – blessed and strengthened in your love; your thoughts always for each other; your plans mutual; your joys and sorrows shared. Every time you light a candle, remember the brightness and the joy of this day. And like the flames of these candles, may there always be evidence of your love, may it lighten any dark times, and may everyone around you feel its warmth.

Unity Sand Ceremony (including one child in the ceremony)

Celebrant (addressing guests): The most beautiful example of partnership is the marriage relationship. Often marriage is viewed as a union of two people, but in reality it is much broader. It is the joining and creation of families. Today, as David and Melissa have sealed their commitment to each other with the exchanging of rings, they also make a commitment to Lauren, as they symbolise the joining of their lives as a family through the blessing of a sand ceremony.

You will see that Melissa and David are each holding separate vases of different coloured sand. This represents the individuality of their separate lives and their own individual life stories. There is also a vase of sand for Lauren, to recognise the significant role that she has as a deeply loved individual within the family.

To symbolise the importance of each of you as individuals, the sand will be layered into the unity vase. Then you will pour more sand in together, showing how your lives have joined, like the grains of sand mixed together, and bonding you all as one united whole.

I start by pouring in some sand which represents the beliefs and values which you hold and share, and which are the foundation of your relationship.

Celebrant pours in neutral sand.

David and Melissa, I invite you to step forward, to pour into the unity vase the sand that symbolises your individuality. David, sand that represents you, all that you were, all that you are, and all that you will ever be. And Melissa, sand that represents you, all that you were and all that you are, and all that you will ever be.

David takes one vase of sand and pours half into the large vessel.
Melissa takes the other vase of sand and pours half into the large vessel.

Celebrant: I now invite Lauren to pour your sand – on top of the firm foundation that is the love of David and your mum, demonstrating your importance within the family, and the special place you have in their lives.

Lauren pours sand into the vessel.

Celebrant: And now I invite David and Melissa and Lauren to pour their remaining sand together.

Melissa, David, and Lauren pour sand together into the vase – the sand mixing as it pours…

Celebrant: And finally, I seal the relationship, covering it with this layer of sand which represents all of you here – the friends and community who are so important in supporting Melissa and David in their marriage, supporting all of them as a family, and holding them in love.,

Celebrant pours remaining sand into the unity vase.

Celebrant: See how the elements of sand are mixed. Just as the sand for each individual has been poured into one container, your lives are joined together as one. Just as these grains of sand can never be separated and poured again into the individual containers, so is the bond for you all. May your love, like the sand, be eternal and inseparable.

Cake Ceremony

Celebrant: Most people make arrangements for their wedding cake several weeks before their wedding, but Sid and Martha have decided to put their skills as bakers to good use, and make a cake as part of their ceremony.

Celebrant: Like all good marriages, it starts with preparation:

Martha and Sid collect a bowl, a whisk and a cake tin.

Celebrant: Then the important ingredients are added – flour which represents the hard work which Sid and Martha put into making a success of their lives; sugar to add sweetness to every day; butter to smooth their path through life; baking powder to give them a lift if ever they are down; and chocolate for those exquisite moments of indulgence. Three eggs are added, to bind them forever in a delightful mix.

During this, Sid and Martha pour and mix the ingredients, and put them into a cake tin for baking.

Celebrant: A marriage doesn't exist in isolation, but it flourishes and is encouraged by all those who support it. This afternoon, Sid and Martha appreciate the support of those who will bake the cake for them, in the same way as they appreciate the warmth and love that surrounds them in this ceremony now. And they want you to share in their happiness, so later today, you should all receive a portion of the chocolate cake – eat it and remember all the love, care, and joint effort which has gone into its making.

Note: To add to the cake theme, Martha and Sid also chose the following reading:

A Good Wedding Cake

4lb of love.

1lb butter of youth.

½lb of good looks.

1lb sweet temper.

1lb of blindness of faults.

1lb of self forgetfulness.

1lb of pounded wit.

1lb of good humour.

2 tablespoons of sweet argument.

1 pint of rippling laughter.

1 wine glass of common sense.

1oz modesty.

Put the love, good looks, and sweet temper into a well-furnished house. Beat the butter of youth to a cream, and mix well together with the blindness of faults. Stir the pounded wit and good humour into the sweet argument, then add the rippling laughter and common sense. Work the whole together until everything is well mixed, and bake gently forever.

Salt Ceremony

Celebrant: As we come to the close of this wedding ceremony today, we have a very special gesture.

We have here two containers of salt. This substance was once more highly valued than gold. It acts as a preservative and purifier, and prevents decay and corruption. It also symbolises how love and marriage can enhance every aspect of the day-to-day life of a couple, in the same way as a pinch of salt can bring out the flavour of food.

Nicola and Simon will each take a pot of salt – these represent their individuality, and their hopes, dreams, and desires for their marriage. They will pour it into the same container, symbolising how their lives have become shared.

Simon and Nicola each pour salt into one central container.

Celebrant: It would be impossible to take this pot of salt, and to separate out the grains of salt which were brought by Nicola from those that were brought by Simon. In the same way, now that Simon and Nicola have made their commitments and exchanged their marriage vows, they are forever joined and their lives cannot be separated.

So, Simon and Nicola, may your love be preserved, and your lives enhanced.

May you have happiness, and may you find it making one another happy.

May you have love, and may you find it in loving one another.

Ladies and gentlemen, please be upstanding, as it is my pleasure and privilege to introduce to you for the first time:

Simon and Nicola, as Mr and Mrs Salt

(this truly was the groom's family name)

GESTURES OF COMMITMENT

Fisherman's Knot

Celebrant: Today is a day of great celebration and laughter and joy. But this portion of the day also has a serious meaning – it is about family and friends coming together, and witnessing the promises that Tommy and Elin will make to each other. Their relationship stands, not only by the authority of the law, but by the strength and the power of the trust and love that they have in one another. There are many gestures which symbolise the relationship between two people, and I'd like to share with you the story of the True Lover's Knot:

Around the turn of the nineteenth century, an art form arose from the traditions of deep-water fishermen. That art form was knotting. (Celebrant holds up rope.) Sailors used rope like this to create a variety of knots. Some knots were purely for practical use; some knots were created for decorative use. And some knots were used to signify meaning. One knot that arose during this time was the Lover's Knot. The true lover's knot is straightforward. It is made up of two overhand knots, linked together, much like the 'true-lovers' are in their hearts. Although the fisherman's knot is one of the simplest to tie, it is also one of the sturdiest. As stress is applied, the knot becomes ever stronger, and the bond will not break.

In days of old, a sailor would tie the knot loosely, and send it to his 'intended' back home. Upon receiving it, the woman could either untie it, meaning the sailor shouldn't show his face around the next time he was in port; or she could send it back leaving it loose, the way she received it, meaning the sailor would be welcomed home, but he better be on his best behaviour; or she could tighten the knot before returning it, meaning the sailor should hurry his way home to marry her.

Celebrant: Tommy, today you are asking Elin to marry you. So take this cord, which represents the bond between you, and tie the knot which signifies your intentions for your gathered friends and family to see.

Tommy ties the knot and hands the rope to Elin.

Celebrant: Elin, will you tighten the knot to represent how you will hold his heart tight to yours.

Elin tightens knot and hands rope to Celebrant.

Celebrant holds knot up for all to see.

Celebrant: We can see by this knot before us that you, Elin and Tommy, both share the same intentions for your marriage, that you will hold each other's heart tight, and form a strong bond from here to forever. I ask that you now pull on this rope to see it strengthen under pressure, while still allowing us to see the individual cords – just as your support of one another as individuals strengthens your union. Let this knot indicate the strength of your love and be a symbol of your unity from this day forward.

Three Stranded Knot - A covenant of commitment

Celebrant: Leanne and Gordon, your wedding ceremony is the most important part of your wedding day. In your ceremony, you commit your life to the person that you love, creating a life-long bond. It is also a time to worship God and thank Him for bringing you together, and supporting you with His blessings in getting you to this new point in your journey through life.

You have stated your desire to keep God at the centre of your wedding ceremony and also at the centre of your marriage. As you think back on your wedding ceremony, it will remind you of how God is intimately involved in your marriage, binding you together with His love, and so we tie the three stranded knot.

You have chosen a verse from Ecclesiastes 4:12: 'Though one may be overpowered, two can defend themselves. But a cord of three strands is not quickly broken.'

This passage illustrates the importance of your relationship, believing that couples bound together in Christ are stronger than the individuals themselves. The Bible teaches that God performs a miracle during marriage, uniting you together in a covenant relationship with Him. The Cord of Three Strands is a symbol of that sacred union created today.

The first cord represents the divinity of God. This covenant of your marriage is initiated by God and supported by all His blessings.

The second cord represents the husband. As Gordon loves Leanne, he will demonstrate his great love in the marriage relationship.

The third strand represents the wife. As Leanne honours Gordon, she will nurture and strengthen the marriage relationship.

Gordon and Leanne braid three cords together while the Celebrant reads:

No beginning, never ending

Patterns dancing, weaving, wending

Now entwining, now embracing

Threads of beauty interlacing

Constantly moving, endlessly loving

Inviting, creating, life celebrating

Belonging, believing

The flow of life weaving

Now over, now under

An infinite wonder.

<u>Celtic Handfasting</u>

Celebrant: William and Cecilia are incorporating into their ceremony today, the ancient ritual of Celtic hand-fasting. In Scotland until the mid-1700s, few unions were sanctified in religious buildings. Instead, they were cele-brated by a simple ceremony in which the partners joined hands and made their promises. The couple's hands were bound using fabric from each partner, showing that the marriage is more than a joining of two people; it is the joining of families, and the extension of a community of family and friends. Today, we build upon this tradition, gently wrapping the fabric/ribbons around the clasped hands of Cecilia and William, 'tying the knot' and unit-ing them as a couple.

*There are two pieces of ribbon or fabric, each about
1.5m long – one representing William and his 'clan'
or family, and one representing Cecilia and her clan or
family.*

Cecilia and William, please clasp hands together *(right hand to right hand).*

(Celebrant ties the ribbons around their hands.)

We take these two ribbons and join them, and as these ribbons are tied, so you acknowledge that your lives have become entwined.

William and Cecilia, look at the hands that are hold-ing yours today: These are the hands that will love and cherish you through the years; these are the hands that will work alongside yours, as together you build your future; these are the hands that will give you strength if you struggle through difficult times; these are the hands that will support you and encourage you to follow your dreams; these are the hands that you hold today in joy, and excitement, and hope.

Vows – made while the couple's hands are tied together

Celebrant: Look now upon your hands
One is free and one is tied.
As you are free to love each other
As you are willingly tied in your love for each other.
The knots of your binding are not formed by this ribbon, but instead by your vows. Even as you take your hands from the ribbons, the ties between you remain, and you hold in your own hands the making of your union.

William and Cecilia gently remove their hands from the ribbons which remain tied in a knot.

Celebrant holds up tied ribbons.

Cecilia and William have just tied the knot *(clapping and cheering)*. In the binding of the ribbon, may you remember the binding of your words. May your hands be always clasped in friendship, and your hearts forever joined in love.

Pagan-type Handfasting

I have not included a full Pagan handfasting, since that has a particular form and set of words, which your celebrant will know if you are Pagan. This example was created for a couple who wanted to acknowledge and incorporate some of their Pagan beliefs within a more Western ceremony.

Preparations and arrival

Celebrant: May this space and all that is contained within it and around it be blessed with the gifts of the East: Communication of the heart, mind, and body, fresh beginnings with the rising of each sun, the knowledge of the growth found in the sharing of silences.

May this space and all that is contained within it and around it be blessed with the gifts of the South: Warmth of hearth and home, the heat of the heart's passion, the light created by both to lighten the darkest of times.

May this space and all that is contained within it and around it be blessed with the gifts of the West: The deep commitments of the lake, the swift excitement of the river, the refreshing cleansing of the rain, the all-encompassing passion of the sea.

May this space and all that is contained within it and around it be blessed with the gifts of the North: A firm foundation on which to build our lives, a stable home to which we may always return.

May this space and all that is contained within it and around it be blessed with the gifts of the Centre: Inspiration to formulate ideas, steadfastness and energy to implement plans, and the spirit of love and cooperation which makes it all possible.

Arrival of Susanna and Ronald (together) into the space.

Celebrant: Ronald and Susanna, welcome. We have come here to be part of this intimate and personal ceremony.

You have planned for this time and committed yourself to this ceremony, declaring your intentions for your love and your life. Susanna and Ronald, your lives have crossed, and you have formed eternal and sacred bonds. As you seek to be joined in this union, you should strive to make real the ideals that to you give meaning to this ceremony and to the promises you make. With full awareness, know that within this space you are not only declaring your intent before each other, but you speak that intent also to whatever mysteries are part of your beliefs. The promises made today and the ties that are bound here, greatly strengthen your union and will span the years of your love and the growth of your souls.

Do you still seek to enter this ceremony?

Ronald and Susanna: *We do.*

Celebrant: We are glad to meet here amongst the trees in the presence of Universal love to affirm the commitment of this couple. We honour the elements within and without, and call on them to celebrate the coming together of Ronald and Susanna.

We thank the earth for providing shelter and nourishment
Water for the flow of life itself
Fire for warmth and passion
Air for every breath
Wood for the urge to act

Statement of Intentions

Celebrant: As we move towards our handfasting ritual, we acknowledge that your union joins two people who trust the love they have found. It is a statement to the world that you have found such love, friendship, and support, that you commit to sharing this portion of your lives together. Your commitment is for a year and a day – a symbolic representation of the cycle of the year, and then some more… accepting that we are not the controllers of time, and gracefully accepting the mysteries of life. So, I ask: do you honour each other's path, and affirm that you will uphold the conditions for your joint and individual growth?

Ron and Susannah: *I do.*

Celebrant: Do you promise to love each other through all circumstances?

Ron and Susannah*: I do.*

Handfasting Vows

Celebrant: Susanna and Ronald, please turn to face each other, and clasp hands. As you stand, with hand clasped to hand, you prepare to make your vows to each other.

Celebrant prepares the ribbons.

Ronald and Susanna, will you be each other's faithful partner for as long as love lasts?
Will you be each other's constant friend and one true love?

Both answer: Yes/I will.
First ribbon is placed and the first promise is made.

Susanna and Ronald, do you promise to love each other without reservation?
Will you stand by one another in sickness and in health, in plenty and in need?

Both answer: Yes/I will.

Second ribbon is placed and the second promise is made.

Ronald and Susanna, will you stand together in times of sorrow and times of joy?
   Will you share the burdens of each, so that your spirits may grow in your relationship?

Both answer: Yes/I will.

Third ribbon is placed and the third promise is made.

Susanna and Ronald, will you share your laughter?
   Will you look for the brightness in life and the positive in each other?

Both answer: Yes/I will.
Fourth ribbon is placed and the fourth promise is made.

Ronald and Susanna, will you always be open and honest with each other?
   Will you dream together to create new realities and hopes for your relationship?

Both answer: Yes/I will.
Fifth ribbon is placed and the fifth promise is made.

Susanna and Ronald, will you honour each other?
   Will you seek to cherish and strengthen your love?
   Both answer: Yes/I will.

Sixth ribbon is placed and the sixth promise is made.

Ronald and Susanna, will you recognise unity of all things?

Will you accept divine blessing and presence in your lives?

Both answer: Yes/I will.

Seventh ribbon is placed and the seventh promise is made.

Binding of all promises

Celebrant: This is a union between two people, of male and female, but it is also reflects many other aspects that are important in your life, which become bound together in your relationship. The ribbons are made of many colours which cross over and create new patterns and shades. This is a representation of both your individuality and your unity, and all the different strands that combine to create your life. The ribbons are a symbol of the life that you have chosen to create together. As they are tied, so you acknowledge that your lives have become entwined.

Celebrant ties the ribbon around your hands.

Ronald and Susanna, as your hands are bound together now, so your lives and spirits are joined in a union of love and trust. Above you are the stars, and below you is the earth. Like the stars, your love should be a constant source of light, and like the earth, a firm foundation from which to grow.

Celebrant: Susanna and Ronald,

May you continue to grow closer within the gentle embrace of love

May your union be a secure place to rest and shelter from life's changes

May you always be kind to each other

May your union be the ground from which you are free to express the purpose of your soul

May the loving energy which brought you together, keep you.

Each of these blessings emphasises those things which will help you build a happy and successful union. Yet they are only tools. Tools which you must use together in order to create what you seek in your relationship. May you be blessed with the desire and intention to re-create your union daily.

The Oathing Stone

Celebrant: While Chris and Julie exchange their vows, they will place their hands on an Oathing Stone. It is part of Celtic folklore that touching the stone during the reading of the vows casts them into the stone and makes them permanent.

When each guest arrived, you were given a stone to hold in your hand during the wedding ceremony. Julie and Chris chose these stones as symbols of your special relationship, love, good wishes, and heartfelt blessings to them. The stones will serve as a lasting reminder of your presence at their wedding, and of the love that surrounded them on their special day. As you hold the blessing stone tightly in your hand, please reflect for a moment your wishes for this couple for love, good health, prosperity, and contentment.

Following the ceremony, Chris and Julie will invite you to place the stones, with your personal blessing for them as a newly-married couple, onto the cairn that they have been building over the past few days. *[alternatively, your guests could place the stones in a jar for you to keep]*

Julie and Chris place their hands on the Oathing Stone and make their vows.

Celebrant: Listen to the words of a special Celtic Blessing for the bride and groom:

High up above you are the stars,
All around you is the air and the wind
Look down, too, at the stones beneath your feet.
As time passes, remember...
Like the stars, your love should be constant and bright
Like the air, your love should be fresh and dynamic
Like the stones, your love should be solid and firm and stable.
Let the brightness of the stars guide your hopes and dreams
Let the powers of the wind allow you to grow and change
with ease,
Let the strength of the stones bring the determination to
succeed.
Have patience with each other,
For stars may disappear from sight, yet they
remain in the galaxy
For storms may come, and yet they pass by
leaving sunshine and freshness
For stones may feel rocky and hard, and yet
they enable you to take the next step forward
So delight in the brightness of your future.
Breathe in the warmth of affection.
Stand firm in your love.
Now and always!

GESTURES OF TRUST AND SHARING

Sample Quaich ceremony

Marriage is a celebration of two people who are making the commitment to share everything that life brings to them. To symbolise this commitment today, Hal and Louise are going to share a drink from the quaich. It is an old Scottish custom that when two clans or families met together, they would share a drink. Sharing a cup was seen as a sign of trust between the people drinking from it – because it is offered and taken with both hands, the drinker could not hold a weapon at the same time, and the sharing of the drink was also a guarantee that it hadn't been poisoned! It demonstrated that the people involved had only good intentions for their relationship, and intended to cause the other no harm or upset or difficulty. As a wedding ritual, sharing a drink from this quaich symbolises the trust that Louise and Hal have in each other, it shows their positive intentions towards each other for all time, and their commitment to share everything that life brings to them.

Celebrant pours whisky into the quaich and holds it up.

Celebrant: The years of your life together are like a cup of liquid poured out for you to drink. This quaich contains within it a drink that has some sweet properties – symbolic of happiness, joy, hope, peace, love, and delight. The same drink also has some bitter properties that are symbolic of life's trials and challenges. As you share the drink, you undertake to share all that the future may bring. All the sweetness that life may hold for each of you will be even sweeter because you drink it together.

Whatever challenges it may contain will be less difficult because you share them and face them together.

Hal and Louise, drink to the love you've shared in the past, drink to your love in the present and acknowledge that your lives have become one, and drink to your love in the future and forever more!

Louise and Hal drink from the quaich.

Celebrant: As you have shared the drink from a quaich, so may you share your lives. May you explore life's mysteries together and find life's joys heightened, its bitterness sweetened, and all of your life enriched by the love of family and friends.

Lock and Key/Treasure Box

(The couple had a box which contained a bottle of wine. They used a padlock locked by two separate keys.)

Celebrant: The American physician and poet Oliver Wendell Homes wrote: 'Love is the master key that opens the gates of happiness.'

Today Isla and Gibson are using keys to symbolise their love and the happiness that they have brought to each other's lives. Once a couple close a padlock together, just as the lock cannot be unlocked, nor can their love and commitment to one another. This ritual symbolises how Gibson and Isla have opened their hearts, and their lives to one another.

The keys to love are many, it is the ability to understand not only the words we say but also those unspoken gestures, the little gifts in life that say so much, without thought of return, the giving in but never giving up, the acceptance of one another's shortcomings, and together facing good fortunes as well as bad. Isla and Gibson, as you join your separate lives into one, I invite you to lock your locks together as a symbol of your commitment to each other.

Isla and Gibson lock the casket.

Celebrant: I know that Gibson and Isla have debated long and hard about what to do with the keys from today. They each have worries that one might be lost in a 'man-drawer', and the other somewhere in the depths of a handbag, so you have decided to put them in a place of mutual safe-keeping. They have created this frame with a glass front, into which they will place the keys. This frame is like one that you see on a train or in a public place – overwritten with the words 'In case of emergency – Break glass'.

Gibson and Isla place the keys into a frame.

Celebrant: As these locks will be locked together, so will your love and commitment to each other. The locking demonstrates you are forever joined together in a lifelong partnership, a promise between you both that you will make decisions together. It will represent your intention to keep each other safe in good times and in bad. And yet it will acknowledge that there are times when you decide together to smash the glass and drink the wine which will remind you of today. Let these keys remind you that you are joining your hearts and souls together for a lifetime.

[then Gibson's brother read this…]

The Key To Love

The key to love is understanding...
The ability to comprehend not only the spoken word,
but those unspoken gestures,
the little things that say so much by themselves.

The key to love is forgiveness...
to accept each other's faults and pardon mistakes,
without forgetting, but with remembering
what you learn from them.

The key to love is sharing...
Facing your good fortunes as well as the bad, together;
both conquering problems, forever searching for ways
to intensify your happiness.

The key to love is giving...
without thought of return,
but with the hope of just a simple smile,
and by giving in but never giving up.

The key to love is respect...
realising that you are two separate people,
with different ideas;
that you don't belong to each other,
that you belong with each other, and share a mutual bond.

The key to love is inside us all...
It takes time and patience to unlock all the ingredients
that will take you to its threshold;
it is the continual learning process
that demands a lot of work...

but the rewards are more than worth the effort...
and that is the key to love.

Food Sharing Ceremony

(Carla and Ian have Buddhist interests, they are both cooks, and including food in their ceremony was important.)

Celebrant: Today, as we celebrate the marriage of Ian and Carla, we acknowledge the past, the present, and the future – the events and delight of Carla and Ian's court-ship; the ceremony we have here today; and the wonders and mysteries of what is still to come. This mirrors Carla and Ian's approach to the food they eat – gratitude for the earth, the work and labour that brings food to our table; the joy of taste and flavour in the present moment; and the future health and abundance that we anticipate.

Carla and Ian have made little cakes for each of you – they have a layer of oats, representing the growth of the seasons, a layer of sweetness symbolising all that is good and sweet about today, and a little surprise on the top to transport you to the future. _[they had topped the cake with 'space dust'/popping candy]_

However, for Ian and Carla, sharing food is not simply about taking what you want, it is about offering some-thing to another person – selflessly. So as Carla and Ian take their cakes, they appreciate the past, celebrate today, and symbolise their intentions for the future:

Ian: _I receive this food in gratitude to all beings, and thankfulness for all who made it possible._

Carla: _I celebrate that today we share with all those we love._

Ian: *I commit that for the future – whatever I have, I will give you the first bite (offers his cake to Carla).*

Carla: *I commit that for the future – whatever I have, I will give you the first bite (offers her cake to Ian).*

Celebrant: *(Buddhist thanksgiving)*
We receive this food in gratitude to all beings
Who have helped to bring it to our table
And vow to respond in turn to those in need
With wisdom and compassion.

GESTURES OF LOVE AND PROTECTION

Tree planting

Here is an excerpt from the ceremony of Dan and Catriona. Their wedding was in a wood, and they had chosen an oak sapling to plant.

Celebrant: As we stand here today, Dan and Catriona's marriage is like the roots of this young, yet resolute sapling. As Cat and Dan have found each other and chosen to share their lives together, the roots of this tree will burrow through the mysterious unknown underground. Unseen, they will find the elements that sustain them and allow them to grow. Intertwined, supporting and being supported by each other, the roots of the relationship that support Dan and Catriona will grow stronger in their union into endless depths.

Above ground, their love will be nurtured by your love, support, and attention, in the same way as branches and leaves are nurtured by sunlight.

Catriona and Dan plant the tree sapling and pour water onto the ground.

Celebrant: Love is the core of our experience and emotion. It is the root of all we do. Love enriches our experience, and fills our lives with meaning. It gives us a firm base from which to grow, to learn, and change. Let your relationship and your love for each other be like this tree you plant today. Let it grow tall and strong. Let it stand tall during the harsh winds and rains and storms, and come through unscathed. Like a tree, your marriage must be resilient. It must weather the challenges of daily life and the passage of time.

Celebrant: Like the tree you are planting, marriage requires constant nurturing and nourishment.

Dan and Catriona (*together*): We water this sapling, and day by day we will remember to nourish each other, with words of encouragement, trust, and love.

Love is enough: though the World be a-waning,
And the woods have no voice but the voice of complaining,
Though the sky be too dark for dim eyes to discover
The gold-cups and daisies fair blooming thereunder,
Though the hills be held shadows, and the sea a dark wonder,
And this day draw a veil over all deeds pass'd over,
Yet their hands shall not tremble, their feet shall not falter;
The void shall not weary, the fear shall not alter
These lips and these eyes of the loved and the lover.

Rose Ceremony

Celebrant: In the elegant language of flowers, red roses are a symbol of love, and the giving of a single red rose is a clear and unmistakable way of saying the words 'I love you'. For this reason, it is fitting that the first gift you exchange as husband and wife should be the gift of a single red rose.

Joe presents a red rose to Frances.

Frances, take this rose as a symbol of my love. It began as a tiny bud and blossomed, just as my love has blossomed and grown for you.

Frances presents a red rose to Joe.

Joe, take this rose as a symbol of my love. Once closed so tightly, it opened to the warmth of the sun, just as my heart has opened to the warmth of your kindness.

Joe and Frances place the roses together in a vase.

Celebrant: We have here roses which represent love and beauty, and yet they have been handled with care because on the stem there are thorns. In accepting the rose from each other, you are accepting the good with the bad, acknowledging the reality that marriage is no fairy-tale.

In every marriage there are times when there may be thorns alongside the flowers. Sometimes it is difficult to find the right words, and the ones we love the most are the ones we can most easily hurt. There are times when it may be difficult to say 'I'm sorry' or 'I forgive you' or 'I need you' or 'I'm hurting'. So I would also ask that wherever you may make your home, that you choose a special spot. And at those times when words fail, that you leave a red rose at that spot you have both selected – a rose that will say what matters more than all other words... 'I still love you'.

Celebrant: Joe and Frances, in remembrance of this day, I would ask as a reaffirmation of your love and of the vows you have spoken here today, that you give each other a single red rose each year on your anniversary.

Frances and Joe: *We will.*

Joe's brother then sang:

> *O my Luve's like a red, red rose,*
> *That's newly sprung in June:*
> *O my Luve's like the melodie,*
> *That's sweetly play'd in tune.*
>
> *As fair art thou, my bonnie lass,*
> *So deep in luve am I;*
> *And I will luve thee still, my dear,*
> *Till a' the seas gang dry.*
>
> *Till a' the seas gang dry, my dear,*
> *And the rocks melt wi' the sun;*
> *And I will luve thee still, my dear,*
> *While the sands o' life shall run.*
>
> *And fare-thee-weel, my only Luve!*
> *And fare-thee-weel, a while!*
> *And I will come again, my Luve,*
> *Tho' 'twere ten thousand mile!*

GESTURES FROM TRADITION, CULTURE and RELIGION

Mexican Lasso/Lazo Ritual

The Lazo Ceremony – two Souls United in the 'Lasso' of Everlasting Love!

Alejandro and Sofia have exchanged their vows. They kneel on the ground.

The celebrant, or family members, drape a lasso made of rope, flowers, silk or beads around the couple in a figure of eight – symbolic of 'infinity' or 'eternity'.

After the prayer and before either attempts to rise, at the end of the ceremony, the lasso is removed.

Celebrant: Sofia and Alejandro have chosen to incorporate the Lasso ritual into their wedding ceremony today. The Lasso is a wedding ritual in which the couple are bound together with a ceremonial rosary. Lassoing is a declaration of intent, where the bride and groom clearly state that they are marrying of their own free will.

With full awareness, know that within this Lasso you are declaring your intent to be bound together in your marriage. Will you honour and respect one another, and seek to never break that honour?

Alejandro and Sofia: *We will.*

Celebrant: Sofia and Alejandro, as you are bound together now, so, too, your lives are joined in a union of love for all time.

As you begin your journey down the road of life together, we know not what lies ahead, for the road has many turns and bends. This lasso ties you together in love, helping you to respect each other's likes and dislikes, opinions and beliefs, hopes, and dreams, and fears, even though you may not always understand them.

It binds you as you learn from each other, and to help each other to grow mentally, emotionally, and spiritually.

It forms a visible and never-ending sign that no matter what happens, you will hold onto each other and know that things have a way of working out for the good.

And so it is.

A Greek Crowning Ceremony

The Betrothal

We are including in our ceremony today the Greek wedding traditions of Betrothal and Crowning. The focal point of the Betrothal is the exchange of rings, so I now invite the best man, or Kumbaro, to come forward with the rings. The Kumbaro (Panagiotis) will bless the rings and they will be exchanged three times.

Celebrant *(in English):* Vasileios is betrothed to Colette in the name of the Father, the Son, and the Holy Spirit.

Kumbaro *(in Greek)):* Vasileios is betrothed to Colette in the name of the Father, the Son, and the Holy Spirit. Vasileios is betrothed to Colette in the name of the Father, the Son, and the Holy Spirit.

Vasileios is betrothed to Colette in the name of the Father, the Son, and the Holy Spirit.

Exchange of rings.

The Crowning and Ceremonial Walk

In Greek Orthodox traditions, the bride and groom are regarded as part of the royal family of God, and are crowned king and queen of their own dominion, their new fellowship and family. So I now invite Panagiotis to come forward with the stephana. These wedding crowns symbolise the glory and honour that is bestowed upon them by God, and the ribbon between the two stephana symbolises the unity of Vasileios and Colette. Panagiotis will bless the crowns, place them on the heads of Colette and Vasileios, and exchange them three times. This will be followed by the ceremonial walk around the altar. The bride and groom will take their first steps together into their married life, three times around this table, recognising the Holy Trinity and their happiness at the union of these two families.

Celebrant _(in English):_ The servant of God, Vasileios, takes as his crown the servant of God, Colette, in the name of the Father, the Son, and the Holy Spirit.

Panagiotis _(in Greek):_ The servant of God, Vasileios, takes as his crown the servant of God, Colette, in the name of the Father, the Son, and the Holy Spirit.

Exchange of stephana and Ceremonial walk – three times around the altar.

Jumping the Broom

Celebrant: Ben and Kelly-Ann have just pledged themselves to one another, recognising their union comes with responsibilities to be diligent and responsible householders. They understand a marriage is not just a uniting of two hearts and souls as one, but the creation of a new family with obligations and responsibilities to one another, their families, and the community.

At this time, I would like to invite Kenny and Sid to come forward to represent Kelly-Ann and Ben's families. Will you each please hold one end of this broom, as a gesture of support for your children's marriage? By serving as anchors, these two families provide Ben and Kelly-Ann with the security of unconditional love, and a source of tradition, heritage, and history.

Ben and Kelly-Ann, a broom is an instrument of labour, reminding us a successful marriage entails hard work as well as effortless passion. As a broom sweeps away all that is unwanted in our homes, may you endeavour to sweep away any troubles that threaten your union. Not sweep it into the corners, but sweep it right out of your lives.

This broom represents the strength, love, togetherness, loyalty, and respect essential for a successful marriage.

Sid and Kenny place the broom on the ground in front of Ben and Kelly-Ann.

Ben and Kelly-Ann, may this broom always remind you of your new life and commitment to each other. Display it proudly in your home. Whenever you see it, may it be a joyous reminder of the way you felt today, your wedding day. May it inspire a sense of honour and respect for your family, and a legacy you now share and create anew today. You may now leap into your new life as husband and wife.

Kelly-Ann and Ben leap across the broom.

Note

Of course, there are many other cultures and rituals not covered here. However, to be authentic in the writing of this book, I have only included rituals, gestures, and ceremonies that I have held, or seen, or participated in. I have read of some wonderful rituals, and I have heard tales of singing and dance and ritual. I would love to work with couples getting married who have such plans, but I have to be honest and include only what I have experienced so far.

Appendix 2

50 Important Questions

You might have read the whole book or you might have dipped in and out, but these are the 50 most important questions as you plan your ceremony. There may be simple answers to some questions; they may not be relevant to the ceremony you are planning; or perhaps you are having a very small event. For other questions, you might want to refer back to the source chapters in more depth.

What I am certain of is that if you and your fiancé(e) work through all of these together, you will be planning a wonderful and personal ceremony that you can both enjoy.

Chapter 1: The Arrival

1. Who is in your bridal party? What order will they arrive in?

2. Do you need a seating plan for the first couple of rows?

3. How will the ceremony space be prepared or decorated?

4. Where will you stand for the ceremony? Will you sit during any of it?

5. Who can you trust to make sure everything goes smoothly on the day?

Chapter 2: Welcome and Opening Words

1. What is most important about your ceremony? Is there a feeling or mood that you want to capture?

2. Are there lines from songs or words from a film or book which sum up how you feel about each other?

3. Where have your guests travelled from? Do you want to make any special mentions of people or places? Are there loved ones who can't be with you? If your families will be present, is there anything that it would be helpful for your celebrant to be aware of, either within your families, or between your families?

4. Do either of you have children (if so, what are their names and ages)? Will they attend the wedding? Would you like them to be involved in the ceremony in any way?

5. Is there a belief system that is important to either of you? Are you religious, non-religious, humanist, spiritual, or not sure? Do you want anything of those beliefs reflected in your ceremony?

6. Would you like to include a prayer, a non-religious blessing, or prayerful thoughts during your ceremony? Are there terms such as God, Love, Divine presence, spirit of love, Angels, universal connection, shared humanity, eternal love, etc. which are meaningful for you, or which you would prefer to avoid?

7. If you do not want a prayer or blessing, would you like an opportunity for people to be still and be quiet, to collect their thoughts, and to focus on you/marriage/ the meaning of love? Or to (silently) offer their thoughts of love, good wishes, and blessing for your future?

8. Is there a dominant belief system held by the majority of your family and friends attending the wedding? Is it different from your own? Is it important to have an acknowledgement of the variety of faiths and beliefs?

Chapter 3: Your Story

1. How, when, and where did you meet? What attracted you to each other? When did you first feel that you were in love?

2. How did your relationship strengthen and develop? What can you say about how it's been since you got together up until now? What are the best things that have happened? Any amusing incidents? Have there been challenges during your time together?

3. What do you love, appreciate, and admire most about each other? What is the most important aspect of the relationship, for each of you?

4. What are the three best things about your partner? These can be funny or serious, they don't have to be complex.

5. What does it mean to you both to be getting married? Why is it important to you?

6. When/where did you get engaged (if you did)? Was it a surprise or a joint decision? Do you have a proposal story?

7. What strengths and qualities are each of you bringing to the marriage? Are there challenges to overcome?

8. How do you hope your future married life together will be? Will anything change, or are there things that you hope will never change? Do you have any specific plans?

9. Which values would you like to base your married life on? What are the fundamental issues which underpin your relationship? List three values each, and give your definitions of what you personally mean by them (they could be the same).

Chapter 4: The Vows and Promises

1. Are there important words to include in your vows?

2. Looking through various examples, do you have favourite lines, phrases, words, styles?

3. Will your vows be traditional, contemporary, something original, humorous?

4. Will you read you vows, repeat them after the celebrant, remember them? Perhaps a mixture for different sections?

Chapter 5: Exchanging Rings or Other Tokens

1. Will you exchange rings? One each?

2. Who will be responsible for bringing them during the ceremony?

3. Are there important words to include in the exchange?

4. Looking through various examples, do you have favourite lines, phrases, words, styles?

5. If you are not exchanging rings, will you exchange something else of significance?

Chapter 6: Choosing Music

1. Do you have a favourite song or favourite music artists?

2. What type of music suits the venue and the style of your wedding?

3. Will you have live music or recorded music?

4. Options for arrival music and recessional music?

5. Will there be other music during the ceremony (hymns, song recital or instrumental, communal singing, music during the signing of the legal paperwork)?

6. Who will be in charge of music co-ordination on the day?

Chapter 7: Choosing Readings

1. Do you have favourite poems or books, favourite authors and poets, favourite song lyrics?

2. What type of reading suits the style of your wedding?

3. Who would like to read? Who would YOU like to read?

Chapter 8: Symbolic Gestures

1. Do you want to include a symbolic gesture or ritual?

2. Which sentiments would you like to celebrate? Unity, commitment, trust and sharing, love and protection; or other family or cultural traditions?

Chapter 9: Involving Others

1. Are there important people who should be involved in your ceremony? Children, family members, friends?

2. Do you want all your guests to participate in something – individually or together?

3. Are you combining this ceremony with any other celebration?

Chapter 10: Creating a Stunning Finish

1. Will you kiss?

2. Do you want to include any closing rituals, blessings or readings?

3. How do you want to be introduced? Mrs and Mrs, Husband and Wife, Bride's name and Groom's name?

4. Are there specific instructions for your guests on leaving the ceremony? Photos, confetti, champagne drinking, buses to other venues, signing the guest book?

And finally......

1. Is there anything else (anything at all) that it would be helpful for your celebrant to know?

P.S. One of my colleagues held a dual ceremony – the legal ceremony in Edinburgh for Scottish guests and then a duplicate ceremony in India for Indian guests. The two ceremonies had the same structure and words, except that in India there was also a ceremonial elephant – quite a surprise to my colleague, who doesn't usually ask how many elephants will be there! ☺

Final Thoughts
by celebrant Angie Alexandra

I'm delighted to contribute some of my own thoughts and stories to this book and to endorse many of the suggestions Jane has made. I've included some pointers about deciding on the kind of ceremony you want and the important considerations when choosing your celebrant, and I've also described a few examples of the things which, in my experience, really help to make a wedding ceremony successful. Like Jane, I regularly officiate at wedding ceremonies and I also have personal experience as an individual getting married and making the right choices, and of many of the different types of ceremony available. My own wedding ceremony solutions were so unusual – not many people can claim to have been married by a registrar, a vicar, an interfaith minister, a group of friends, and a celebrant! Not all at once I hasten to add!

I've been married twice and my first marriage was in England many years ago at a time when we had two choices for our marriage – by either a Registrar or a Church Minister. As my ex-husband was Muslim, my family's local church was not an option for him. We discovered that if we had a ceremony in the mosque it would not be legally recognised, so we settled for a short civil ceremony held by a registrar in a hotel. By the time I remarried in 2013 to an Aussie/Scot, there was so much more choice, and we ended up having four very different ceremonies to accommodate both our wishes, and the practical reality of having family and friends in England and Australia most of whom were unable to make the journey to Scotland.

My husband Will and I decided to have an intimate and personal, sacred ceremony just for ourselves, in a holiday cottage on the West Coast of Scotland. This included the legal aspect and was created and led by our four closest friends, all interfaith ministers. With our own needs so beautifully met we could easily have stopped there, however, we knew our wider community of friends would have been hurt and disappointed not to celebrate with us, so the following month we had a second ceremony open to everyone in the village where we live in Scotland. Three hundred people gathered in our local community hall for a creative and alternative ceremony led by an interfaith minister colleague. The following month we travelled to England and enlisted the services of the vicar of the village church where I grew up, to hold a traditional church blessing with my family; then as we had made the effort for the English side of the family, we felt we needed to do the same for the Australian side of the family, so we concluded our nuptials by travelling to Australia for a celebrant led ceremony in a family member's garden.

We were lucky in that neither of our families put us under pressure to have any of our marriage celebrations held in a certain way, and yet I'm well aware that's not the case for some couples who are trying to find a compromise between what they would like, and what their family would like for them, and to find a solution in just the one ceremony. Sometimes couples seek a way to acknowledge and respect some of the religious, spiritual and cultural traditions and beliefs they grew up with, most often to honour the wishes of dearly loved family members, but they don't want their whole ceremony to revolve around one particular culture or tradition. With a little forethought, a tolerant legal framework and a supportive celebrant, finding the right compromise need not be an issue.

In my own wedding celebrations the size of the group and different cultures, traditions and beliefs, all had a bearing on how we celebrated. Our tiny legal ceremony was bespoke and just for us, and then our other ceremonies were tailored to our guests and locations. We thought carefully about how to create roles for each family member, we invited friends to be involved, and we created personal ceremonies which engaged the different groups of guests at each event. It was important to us, as it is for many couples getting married, that we should respect everyone present, regardless of difference in individual belief, and to explore ways of welcoming everyone with sensitive and inclusive wording.

During the months leading up to my ceremonies, I had the opportunity be 'the client' and to experience how each officiant or celebrant responded to and supported me. This re-affirmed how I work with clients, and the importance of developing a relationship where you can work closely with your celebrant, being given reassurance, guidance and ideas, as needed, every step of the way. It really high-lighted for me how different individual officiants can be. Even with similar beliefs and training, each celebrant has their own style of communication, self-management, presentation and delivery.

Living and working in Scotland I know that celebrants can get booked up well in advance – particularly for summer weekends – as many couples want to book their preferred officiant early in the process of wedding plan-ning. However, before settling on your celebrant, it's worth considering which elements are going to be important for you to have in your ceremony, to ensure that your choices are not going to be limited along the way in respect of the rituals, readings, vows, and music that you'd like. Depend-ing on their personal beliefs, the organisation they are affiliated with, and the law in different countries/states, some celebrants will not be able to include anything that would be classed as religious or spiritual (for example no hymns or prayers), some will only offer a ceremony which is in line with their religious tradition's stated doctrine, whilst others will be able to offer complete flexibility and freedom.

You may also want to check out the commitment (if any) that you are being asked to make. Find out whether you have to attend services or meetings, if there is an organ-isation which you must join, particular preparations to undertake, and whether there are any specific beliefs you are expected to endorse. It's also a good idea to gain an understanding of the legal process, particularly if you are planning a wedding which is in a country or state where you do not live. In Scotland for example, it's possible for anyone to travel here to be married, but there is an advance legal application process that has to take place between three months and 29 days before the date you intend to marry on. It would be frustrating and disappointing to find you've left it too late to apply for your wedding to be legal.

When considering who will create and hold your ceremony for you, your choice may be limited if you are being married in a particular church, or if the officiant is allocated by the register office. However, if you do have a choice, consider what qualities are important for you to have in a celebrant. Take note of how quickly and helpfully you receive a response to your email or phone call of enquiry; whether you have a choice of meeting face-to-face or being in contact via email, phone, Skype or FaceTime. Do you hope your celebrant will offer ideas for readings, rituals and vows, or are you happy to research these aspects of your ceremony yourself? Will your celebrant support you in the lead-up to your wedding day with pre-marriage counselling, answering questions, holding a rehearsal, or anything else that might be important to you? And always check out whether there are fees for any of these additional supports and services. Although getting married is not a business, it can help if the agreements made with your celebrant are clarified in a business-like way, with the specifics of your booking confirmed in writing, then you can relax knowing your date is securely in their diary and you can tick another box on your 'to do' list.

It's a good idea if you're clear with your celebrant about the initial plans and ideas you have. For example, if you're hoping to have your ceremony outside in a natural place, find out and then let them know if it will involve a walk or trek, and ensure that your celebrant (and your guests!) are willing and able to walk the distance and manage the terrain. If you plan to be outside whatever the weather, are they happy to wrap up warm, or wear a waterproof and wellies, if needed? Is it important to you what your officiant wears? Some ministers and celebrants wear formal robes, and some wear suits or dresses or kilts – will your celebrant give you a choice? I've been invited to hold some ceremonies based on the fact that I look l like a minister in my robe or more like a civil celebrant in a smart dress or suit. I've also worn a traditional Indian Shalwar Kameez in response a couple's request, and on other occasions I've worn jeans (the bride and groom wore jeans too!).

For small ceremonies or if you're planning an elopement, you might seek someone to take care of a few extra things so you don't have to do anything hands-on yourself on the day. If you like this idea, find out whether your celebrant can help – arranging legal witnesses, if needed; putting a bottle of champagne on ice and glasses ready for the end of the ceremony; or bringing along a portable music player. If you would like that kind of additional support, find out if your celebrant is willing to look after you in this way, and check if there is any additional fee for them to do that.

You may find that choosing a celebrant is overwhelming. You will find every faith and belief represented, and every possible character and personality, from officiants who crack a joke every other sentence to those who are more serious in their approach. There will be those who listen well, and those who provide strong direction to do things their way; those who see their work as a vocation, and those who view it primarily as a business; those who are friendly and approachable, and those who clearly enjoy being in a position of authority. Who would you feel most at ease with, and who do you think would really 'get' you, be able to communicate with you, and represent your ideas and wishes during your ceremony? You can't beat meeting the celebrant in person to get a good sense of them, or – failing that – chatting with them on Skype or FaceTime. You might choose according to your budget, the personality of the celebrant, their style of delivery, their willingness to go the extra mile, or you may base your decision on a recommendation from friends or an online forum. Plan ahead as the most popular celebrants will have bookings several years in advance. Your ceremony is an important part of your day and you'll do well to place your ceremony preparations in capable and reliable hands – and your celebrant will do well to remember your ceremony is all about you and it's an honour and privilege to be of service to you.

Creating Really Successful Ceremonies
Case Studies – Angie Alexandra

I do!

One of the shortest and most powerful sentences in the world – 'I do!' – has the potential to set us off on a life-long journey alongside all other married couples on the planet. Yet every couple approaches that journey in their own way, and I'd like to add to Jane's wonderful collection of words and suggestions with a few thoughts about the things which, in my experience, really help to ensure a wedding ceremony goes well.

Planning and Preparation

I can't agree with Jane enough about the importance of thinking about what needs to be done at the ceremony location before the bridal party arrives. When I offici-ate at a wedding, I usually also take on the role of stage manager and production director, in collaboration with venue staff and/or wedding planners, and I arrive early to ensure everything is set up and in place before the ceremony is due to start. Here are the top 10 things that I suggest you and your officiant discuss and decide before-hand to ensure everything runs smoothly:

- If there are several people in the bridal party or if you have complex choreography, a rehearsal can be a good idea. Decide how your bridesmaids and groomsmen are going to sit or stand during the ceremony, and also how they will leave at the end of the ceremony, following behind you as a newly-married couple. Depending on numbers of each, it can be nice for them to pair up to arrive, and/or pair up to walk back down the aisle, and remember that your photographer may be waiting at the end of the aisle to capture important photos of the newly married couple, so the bridesmaids and groomsmen should ensure not to follow too closely on your heels.

- Make sure there is enough space at the front of the room for all your wedding party, for any musicians, and for your photographer and videographer to work – if space is going to be tight, consider having all your bridesmaids and groomsmen sitting during the ceremony.

- Allocate different roles to each bridesmaid – it's not practical to have one attendant hold her own bouquet, and the bridal bouquet, and try to manage a bridal train or veil with her hands full. If you're only having one attendant and she needs to arrange your dress, maybe you could place your bouquet on the legal signing table or hand it to your celebrant, or to another guest.

- Ensure that the ushers know what they're doing, when they are required, and where, so they can welcome guests and guide them to their seats. They should know who will sit on the front row(s), where closest family are placed, and where people with roles during the ceremony will sit. They should encourage guests to take their seats to avoid leaving any gaps at the front or on the aisle.

- Before the ceremony your officiant should check who has the rings, and that the person bringing them knows how to easily access and present them.

- Be clear on who will provide anything needed for a symbolic ritual, where the items will be and who will set them up. I recommend this is done well in advance of the ceremony start time – it's all a bit of a rush if, five minutes before the ceremony is due to begin, the items for the sand ritual are brought in from the groom's car, still sealed in their original wrapping and difficult to open!

- Discuss with your photographer the plans for pre-ceremony shots with the groom's party, for the bride's arrival, and also whether there are any specific instructions for group photos immediately after the ceremony. Your celebrant can make any beginning or ending announcements about where your guests should go, instructions about throwing confetti, or any other requests, such as whether you prefer that guests do or don't take photos or post anything on social media.

- Don't leave it until the last minute to give someone the role of operating the music – choose someone and give them time to familiarise themselves with both the technology and the tracks, when they are being played, and the cues for starting each piece, and also for the ending of each piece which might involve fading out the sound.

- Be clear about whether the bride is planning to arrive on time. It's good to aim to begin reasonably close to the start time shown on your invitations and on your schedule for the day. Of course, there might be unexpected last minute delays, but plan sufficient time for hair and make-up – which can often take longer than expected – and for pre-ceremony photos of the bridal party arriving at the venue, and the bride getting out of the car. The timing and itinerary for your day will have been carefully planned, and lengthy delays can reduce the time allocated for photos after the ceremony, or set the meal back – a point of concern for your caterers who will be trying to do their best for you, and also for you if you have further guests joining you from a particular time in the evening and you need to be on standby to welcome them. A lengthy wait can also be hard for guests if they've taken their seats in readiness for the ceremony beginning on time, but especially hard for the groom – even the calmest person can start to feel nervous if he has a protracted wait with many eyes on him – he may even start to wonder if you're going to show up and I'm sure you don't want to put him through that.

- It's nice if there are tissues on hand for any happy tears. If your bridesmaids' dresses offer no good place to stow tissues, tissues can be wound around their bouquet handles or stems, out of sight behind the flowers. And there should be tissues or handkerchiefs in the groom's pocket or sporran. He can then offer them to his bride if she gets teary during the ceremony (or even use them himself!).

Personalisation

Every couple I have ever had the honour of creating and holding a ceremony for has been unique, and therefore it follows that every ceremony has been unique. I never tire of hearing how a couple met, what first attracted them to one another, and if there was a marriage proposal, what took place. This can help me write a wonderfully personal wedding address, however, I know that not all couples feel comfortable sharing their story with all their guests, and not everyone can find the words to express how they feel about each other. When a couple are happy to have their story acknowledged and told back to them, it can be immensely moving to invite input from close family and

friends, and a great honour for them to contribute in this
way:

> Catherine and Richard nominated people who knew
> them really well who could give me another perspective
> on their journey from meeting, to engagement, to
> the wedding day – Catherine's two best friends, and
> Richard's surrogate parents. I invited them all to tell
> me about the evolution of Catherine and Richard's
> relationship from their viewpoint, and I merged and
> wove together stories of Catherine and Richard as
> teens before they met, then their meeting which was
> quite dramatic and funny, then becoming a couple,
> then how their relationship progressed. I included
> what their friends saw were their best traits, how they
> worked well as a team together – giving several sweet
> anecdotes about everyday life – as well as an account of
> the very romantic and thoughtful proposal. Catherine
> and Richard chose this to be a surprise for them on the
> day, and as they listened they laughed and cried with
> delight!

Making your ceremony personal can also be reflected in
something very unique to you, and the following accounts
describe some of the lovely ways in which personalisation
can happen and give a variety of ideas which are both fun
and moving:

> When Mog and Steve got married on the beach they
> wanted a really fun and up-beat wedding. They gave
> all their guests kazoos and had them all play 'Here
> Comes the Bride' for Mog's arrival. It was wonderful,
> and really set the tone for a relaxed and light-hearted
> ceremony in the sun.

Elizabeth and Larry chose the theme of a hummingbird, and we wove its symbolism – it represents joy, determination, courage and endurance – into the wedding address. It was a small wedding with only a dozen guests, each of whom received a quaich engraved with a hummingbird as a wedding favour, and Liz and Larry also had hummingbirds engraved inside their wedding rings.

Julie's parents had both passed on sometime before her wedding to Joe. Joe and Julie took her parents' wedding rings and had them melted down and made into two new rings. They felt that by renewing the rings in this way, they would invoke the qualities of love and devotion in their marriage – qualities which had been so evident in Julie's parents' marriage. They asked me to make reference to this as I led them into their exchange of rings.

Mary and Lawrence wanted to be both traditional and contemporary in the vows they said to each other. They felt like they wouldn't feel married if they didn't have the chance to say 'I do', but they also wanted to say some personal words to each other which they decided they would prepare separately as a surprise, but still send to me beforehand. We pre-agreed the format and the length that they would work to – somewhere between 75 and 100 words seemed right – and they agreed to each write three sentences which began with 'I pledge . . .'

Elisabeth and Elmer prepared surprise elements for each other – he read a poem, and she sang a song. Elisabeth was a music teacher, so she was in her

element. Elmer knew he couldn't sing well, but he
played to his strength by pre-preparing some sweet
and loving words in the form of a poem. It was very
personal and very creative.

Ritual and Gesture

Jane has been incredibly thorough in what she has said already, and I can only agree that choosing to include meaningful ritual and symbolic gesture in your ceremony can enhance the overall feel of the ceremony, adding a special something to your day. Music and readings are regular inclusions in a ceremony whereas ritual and gesture other than a ring exchange, are less common, but by including them in your ceremony you can draw people in, making words, sentiments and concepts visible and meaningful. Including ritual and gesture in your ceremony allows you and/or others to take part – to hold or create something, to drink or eat something, to participate in some way, and in doing so it can make the moment seem more relevant and engaging for both you and your guests.

Online, you can see and hear video clips from ceremonies taking place all over the world, and you can get lots of ideas which may begin to inspire you. When I meet with a couple to prepare their ceremony, we discuss the rituals that are of interest to them, and then I offer them the chance to see how a ritual feels and how it flows alongside their ceremony. For example, I have several versions of a hand-tying I can run through with a couple; I can set up a unity candle lighting or a sand pouring; I can let the couple drink from a quaich or a goblet. Sometimes a ritual only comes to life through giving it a go and seeing how it can work, so discuss what your officiant can offer –

they might have ideas to excite you or you might come up with something yourself.

Whether you choose to walk in the footsteps of those who have gone before you and include an ancient hand-tying or a sacred candle lighting, or whether you get creative and invent your own symbolic gesture, including an element of ritual can often be one of the most memorable aspects of your ceremony for you and your guests. With a little forward planning and preparation, together, you and your celebrant can make a very special moment.

Being Married

Your wedding day and ceremony will of course be memorable for you, but afterwards what is most important is how you live your lives together, and the words you say as vows during your ceremony can support that.

Jane and I have both been inspired by author and marriage counsellor Gary Chapman and his book The Five Languages of Love. Gary offers a very simple concept which beautifully supports marriage. It's the idea that each individual has his or her own unique combination of ways of feeling loved and expressing love. Some people need to hear that they're loved or to tell their partner they love them; some need to receive gifts to feel loved or to buy presents for their partner; some need gestures of physical affection to feel loved or show love; some need to have things done for them to feel loved or be involved in a loving act of service; and some most feel and show love when spending time with their partner.

So if your partner makes you breakfast in bed on a Sunday and washes your car every weekend, but never tells you he or she loves you and never gives you a gift, and you're someone who needs to hear you're loved, who likes to receive little love tokens, this is really good information to know, so you as different people can best understand one another, live in harmony and stay in communication, thereby giving yourselves the best chance of creating a healthy and happy marriage from the start. As your marriage is a living entity, anything you can do to nourish and feed it is worth an investment of your time.

This kind of detail is not only useful to know, but it can be woven into your vows, and provide a blueprint for how you choose to be in your marriage moment by moment. James and Maureen are now in their seventies and they had an incredibly short and simple personal vow which they still say to each other on a daily basis: 'We must live and die, and it is you I choose to live and die with; head to head, toe to toe, soul to soul, now and forever, amen.' Each morning they gently start their day with the vow, followed by coffee on the balcony of their apartment watching the sun come up (they live in Florida!), sharing an easy companionable silence, and they take the words of their vows with them into their day. I'm really moved by that level of thought, commitment, and the way of using what's actually a very powerful support tool for them as they hear and reaffirm their love and commitment to each other every day, and spend quality time with each other.

Another couple I met was inspired by the idea that the commitment made during a handfasting was initially for a year and a day, then reviewed, then renewed. They allowed this idea to inspire them in a very creative and positive way. They chose to wear very inexpensive rings, and every year on their wedding anniversary, they spend the day reflecting on and talking about the year that has gone by. They give up their old rings by throwing them into the sea. Then they make new vows for the upcoming year and seal their commitment by exchanging new rings.

On the day of your wedding, your vows may be emotive or even humorous in the moment when you share them, but it's how you integrate and live their meaning which is going to count as you go forwards on possibly the greatest adventure of your life, so choose them carefully, they will have as much power as you give them! Your marriage will no doubt bring lots of opportunities for practising and living the aspirations of your 'I do's' and I wish you all the very best – may you have graceful preparations, a beautiful wedding day, and a blessed married life.

Lightning Source UK Ltd.
Milton Keynes UK
UKHW02f0648101018
330261UK00005B/97/P